THIS BOOK
BELONGS TO

....

....

Thank you for Purchasing my book and taking the time to read it from front to back. I am always grateful when a reader chooses my work and I hope you enjoyed it!

With the vast selection available online, I am touched that you chose to be purchasing my work and take valuable time out of your life to read it. My hope is that you feel you made the right decision.

I very much would like to know what you thought of the book. Please take the time to write an honest and informative review on Amazon.com. Your experience and opinions will be of great benefit to me and those readers looking to make an informed choice.

With much thanks.

©COPYRIGHT 2024

The content contained within this book may not be reproduced, duplicated, or transmitted without direct written permission from the author or the publisher. Under no circumstances will any blame or legal responsibility be held against the publisher, or author, for any damages, reparation, or monetary loss due to the information contained within this book. Either directly or indirectly.

Legal Notice:

This book is copyright protected. This book is only for personal use. You cannot amend, distribute, sell, use, quote, or paraphrase any part, or the content within this book, without the consent of the author or publisher.

Disclaimer Notice:

Please note the information contained within this document is for educational and entertainment purposes only. All effort has been executed to present accurate, up-to-date, and reliable, complete information. No warranties of any kind are declared or implied. Readers acknowledge that the author is not engaging in the rendering of legal, financial, medical, or professional advice. The content within this book has been derived from various sources. Please consult a licensed professional before attempting any techniques outlined in this book. By reading this document, the reader agrees that under no circumstances is the author responsible for any losses, direct or indirect, which are incurred as a result of the use of the information contained within this document, including, but not limited to — errors, omissions, or inaccuracies.

Table of Contents

What is Artificial Intelligence	6
The History Of AI	8
Within AI	16
How does artificial intelligence work?	18
Understanding Artificial Intelligence	24
Classification of Artificial Intelligence Styles	27
INTRODUCTION TO MACHINE LEARNING	35
WHAT IS MACHINE LEARNING	36
THE FUTURE OF MACHINE LEARNING	40
Deep Learning	48
The Future of Deep Learning	54
Artificial Intelligence Blending To Other Tech	57
What is Big Data?	59
Analytics of Big Data	66
What is the relationship between AI and Big Data?	73
What is predictive analysis?	75
The Future of Artificial Intelligence	84
MYTHS ABOUT ARTIFICIAL INTELLIGENCE	101
What is the actual effect of artificial intelligence on companies?	108
How have THE corporate sectors been affected?	110
What are the advantages of investing in ai?	116
Advantages and Disadvantages of Artificial Intelligence	120
Application Of Artificial Intelligence In Daily Life	126
Artificial Intelligence for Humanoid Robots	132
Conclusions	136

INTRODUCTION

For a long time, it was thought that artificial intelligence (AI) was a myth, a product of science fiction that would never have come true.

The idea was that machines would never have characteristics that imitate intelligence, an exclusively human trait.

The human brain was understood as two distinct things-analytical, imaginative, and emotional-and the equipment is created.

The first industrial revolutions produced equipment that replaced manual labor, doing the work of many more productive and cost-effective men.

A lot has changed today, and it is already understood that the capacity of computers is much greater. And, in many cases, they are already employed in tasks traditionally seen as "intellectuals."

Does that mean these machines have an intellect? Not because, while the analogy is accurate, the "intelligence" of the machines is very different from ours.

In any case, the main thing is that everybody now knows that artificial intelligence is a reality.

What needs to be done is to expand the understanding of its mechanisms and the understanding of the possibilities it offers.

This is a particular challenge for entrepreneurs and managers, who constantly search for greater efficiency in all industries.

In this section, we're going to talk about the idea and explain how artificial intelligence works.

You'll also hear about examples and ways and models to give it a chance.

CHAPTER 1
WHAT IS ARTIFICIAL INTELLIGENCE

Artificial intelligence is the capacity of artificial devices to act in a manner that resembles human thought.

This means perceiving factors, making choices, and solving problems. At the end of the day, work in a logic that applies to reasoning.

According to the Michaelis dictionary, "Artificial" is something that "was created by man's art or industry and not by natural causes."

On the other hand, intelligence is the "faculty of knowledge, thought, reasoning and interpretation." Or the "set of mental functions that make it easier to comprehend things and reality."

There are two meanings of Psychology for the term "intelligence" in the same dictionary:

Firstly, it is the ability to make the most of the success of a situation and use it in the practice of another task. Secondly, the ability to overcome new situations rapidly and effectively and adapt to them through knowledge gained.

Only the last two concepts make sense when we speak about artificial intelligence, an aspect called machine learning.

It is a discipline of computing that studies ways to make computers more intelligent and able to solve problems in an agile and realistic way. To this end, the field seeks inspiration in human learning and seeks to replicate it artificially.

It is different from the traditional computer programming and training model. These algorithms required human intervention to define the rules formally. The programmers specifically state: "If X, then Y." In contrast, AI systems discover their own ways to draw conclusions based on identifying patterns and detecting data trends.

At the entrance of the algorithm, a large amount of data on the subject to be learned must be trained. Then the algorithm discovers relationships, understands the foundation, and produces output, which is the ability to comprehend what has been transmitted, much as human beings would have done.

Thus, they define their own laws, and even the work of a human being becomes expendable. In one of the following subjects, we'll see exactly how the programmer works. What needs to be clarified now is that this does not require the manual work of writing commands and describing logic in depth.

If programmed computers are not smart but fast, AI computers are capable, intelligent, and fast. Through this, it is possible to tackle a broader range of problems in a number of fields.

As an extremely important field in modernity, AI is not a new sector. Her studies started to deepen in the 1950s. Since then, due to the development and evolution of computers, it has evolved, diversified, and become increasingly productive.

Finally, artificial intelligence is designed such that human-created computers can perform such tasks without human intervention.

And what are the functions? The response to that question is more significant with each passing day. We will try to answer later, providing examples of applications for artificial intelligence.

CHAPTER 2
THE HISTORY OF AI

The theme is so motivating that Hollywood has never stopped talking about it. Since Metropolis, a silent movie from 1927, we have created robots, computers, and programs that function for our own good or in pursuit of destruction. Quickly, you can quote 'Blade Runner: The Android Hunter;' 'AI Artificial Intelligence;' 'She,' a personal assistant with the voice of Scarlett Johansson; the Matrix and Terminator franchises;' 'Me, Robot' based on the important work of Isaac Asimov; and '2001: A Space Odyssey with the threatening HAL 9000.

Ideas related to artificial intelligence are long before the technology that made this possible has appeared. Human beings have always wanted a computer that can do the job of behaving and thinking like us. Research from different fields started to go down that road explicitly during the Second World War.

In 1943, Warren McCulloch and Walter Pitts presented an article that talks for the first time about neural networks, artificial reasoning systems in the form of a mathematical model that mimics our nervous system.

Another critical article of the time is the work of Claude Shannon in 1950 on how to program a computer to play chess with easy yet effective position calculations.

Putting This Into Effect

In the same 1950s, the legendary Alan Turing devised a way to determine whether a computer could be used as a person in a written conversation. This is the Turing test, originally known as The Imitation Game, the title of the film that portrayed the life of a researcher with Benedict Cumberbatch in the leading role.

SNARC was born in 1951, a mathematical operations calculator simulating synapses, which are the relations between neurons. Marvin Minsky, a classmate of the pair of the first paper on neural networks, was the person in charge. And in 1952, Arthur Samuel developed an IBM 701 checkerboard game that continues to improve on its own and becomes a challenge for amateur players.

The Base

Everything we have said so far is very accurate, but it came before the time called a kickoff. Ground zero was at the so-called Dartmouth Conference in 1956. This meeting brought together Nathan Rochester from IBM, Shannon from the chess post, Marvin from SNARC, John McCarthy, and many others. The research area was called artificial intelligence by McCarthy. Even the industry maxim was defined: any aspect of learning or another type of intelligence can be represented so that a computer can be designed to simulate it.

From then on, whoever took part in the congress or liked the proposals came together to make AI get off the ground. The potential was so exciting that private and government agencies invested heavily in the field, including ARPA, the Advanced Projects Research Agency, the same place where the internet was born.

Take a look at the sequence of advances of that period: in 57, Frank Rosenblatt introduced the perceptron. This Transformers Character Name algorithm is a neural network of a layer that classifies results and starts as a computer named Mark 1. As early as 58, Lisp's programming language appeared, which at that time became a staple in Artificial Intelligence systems, and today inspires a whole family of languages.

In 59, we see the word machine learning for the first time, defining a device that gives computers the ability to learn a specific function without being explicitly programmed for it. Essentially, this means feeding a data algorithm so that the computer learns to perform a task automatically.

In 64, he had the world's first chatbot, ELIZA, who spoke automatically, imitating a psychanalyst, using responses based on keywords and syntactic structure. And in 69, the Shakey is shown to be the first robot to combine agility, voice and a certain autonomy of action. It was sluggish and defective, but it worked.

The High And The Low

The field of natural language processing has been one of the most exciting. It is an AI field for understanding human speech. It has many applications, such as translators, generation of text languages, speech recognition, voice processing, and more.

But at the same time, we had high hopes and many academic studies; in reality, all was not as concrete or as quick as predicted.

Robots were not walking around with super-powerful software. That's why, from the middle of the '70s to the beginning of the '80s, we're living in a dark time known as the winter of artificial intelligence, an age of little coverage, expenditure cuts, and low exposure to the field.

The field needed to be reinvented. One of the areas that made this possible was that of advanced systems, first suggested by Edward Feigenbaum in the early 1980s. As the name suggests, they are software that performs complex and unique field operations, performing the role of human beings, but with a much quicker rationale and a much broader knowledge base. These systems bring AI closer to the corporate market, and many sectors realize the utility of smart, oriented computer programs.

Take the example of financial investment. A sophisticated framework helps in the analysis of bank credit risk, risk control. Also, it uses algorithms to boost the performance in stock trading and asset management in the financial market. If you like the topic, Udacity has been involved in trading in collaboration with the management company WorldQuant and Nanodegree in AI, which also involves developing financial models.

The Universe Unified By Artificial Intelligence

But let's go back to the timeline because Japan will go down in history with the so-called fifth generation of computers, an effort by the country to invest in technology and modernize the entire industry from 1982 to the 1990s, including artificial intelligence. On the one side, this placed Japan on the map of new breakthroughs at once and accelerated those industries, such as microprocessors and supercomputers.

But the expenditure was again out of reach, not to mention the introduction of a programming language with little support called Prolog and concepts larger than the power of the CPUs at the time.

A second small AI winter took place in the first half of the 1990s, but soon it was over.

The second half of the 1990s was characterized by a commercial Internet explosion. The networks used AI to develop navigation and indexing systems. Programs that automatically scanned the network and categorized results, such as the Google prototype, were born at that time.

Man X Machine

A natural response to how far this field came in 1997 when the computer beat the man in a chess game. Soviet champion Garry Kasparov was defeated in one of IBM's Deep Blue Machine rounds, in matches that reverberated worldwide. Deep Blue has implemented a method of calculation by brute force that analyzes the possibilities, forecasts the reactions, and proposes the best possible movement. It was evident that we were on the right track.

These robots have also been programmed to support us, as the iRobot, which introduced the first Roomba, proved in 2002. This stand-alone cleaning assistant in your home gives ten to zero robots from decades ago to combine the productivity of the specialization, preset, and positioning sensors working together.

Another strong example was Boston Dynamics in 2005. The AI revolution introduced applications in different industries with the BigDog robot, capable of traveling across terrains that are difficult for humans to reach. Dog forms and humanoids are becoming better at agility and intelligence.

Intelligence On The Wheel

Artificial intelligence has also been researched for use in autonomous cars since around 2005. Their case is very complicated. The platform needs to be linked to the vehicle's multiple sensors and traffic itself, from traffic lights to other cars.

This field may take a few years to grow fully, but we are already tracking some of the findings. Since 2004, DARPA has organized an annual competition called the Grand Challenge, which rewards and pushes autonomous car projects. Several concepts and inventions have emerged.

One of the highlights was Sebastian Thrun, from Stanford University, who won the 2005 competition with a Stanley-based vehicle specializing in high-speed desert crossings. Remember that name because this researcher is going to be interesting in a little while.

It is also the case of Waymo, a subsidiary of Alphabet, owner of Google, which has already carried out multiple experiments on self-propelled cars and aims to make this segment famous by 2020.

Intelligent And Smarter

As of 2008, natural language processing has returned to everything. Google introduced a voice recognition feature on the iPhone for testing, demonstrating the incorporation of AI into the entire ecosystem of the business. In 2011, Apple released a virtual assistant, Siri, which answers questions, searches for you, and even tells jokes. It was followed by Alexa, Amazon, who exploded in popularity, Cortana, Microsoft, and Google Assistant.

Today, Siri is one of the personal assistants on the market.

IBM also made headlines again in 2011 with Watson, a supercomputer and an artificial intelligence network. To demonstrate his full potential, he beat the best players on the Jeopardy TV game. Since then, it has begun to be applied in many fields, such as medicine, law, image recognition, and much more.

Udacity Was Born

Known as the University of Silicon Valley, Udacity emerged in 2011 in this groundbreaking ecosystem in the United States, following an experiment by Stanford University professor Sebastian Thrun alongside Peter Norvig, offering a free online course on "Introduction to Artificial Intelligence."

More than 160,000 students from 190 countries have signed up, and more than 400 have outperformed Stanford students. After this episode, Thrun realized that a technology-based university was needed that would be realistic, affordable, open, and highly successful for the world. Udacity has now arisen.

Advanced Learning

Google took another phase in its AI programs in 2012. Consolidating research technologies in deep learning since 2006, she has trained an algorithm to recognize kittens in YouTube videos.

This profound learning uses neural networks with more layers than the pioneers we discussed, processing more information and making the computer freer to assimilate and classify elements. This is how she performs more complex activities, such as recognizing and cataloging images and videos.

The Complex Division Into Deep Learning Layers

Deep learning can be combined with another process: computer vision, which is designed to allow a machine to handle the acquisition, interpretation, and analysis of images. For example, Affective used this in face recognition to identify emotions in the human face.

In recent years, there have been many achievements of artificial intelligence in the human world. In 2014, Eugene Goostman, a chatbot, managed to win the Turing test and persuaded jurors that he, the program, was actually a human being during a written conversation.

AlphaGo, created by Deepmind, became a master in the Go board game in 2016 and won the category world champion in a series of victories much more remarkable than those in chess years ago since the algorithm learned all the rules and tactics of the game by watching other games and then playing against itself.

CHAPTER 3
WITHIN AI

In reality, we usually just see AI as a simple and interactive GUI (Graphical User Interface), but there's a lot behind it. The construction of artificial intelligence includes a set of algorithms, which are code instructions that must be followed primarily in Python, open libraries with instructions and resources that dictate the actions of the code and the system. This more complicated structure incorporates tools and provides a more realistic path for the project.

Nowadays, we have AI in almost every phase we conduct in electronics. In the organization of playlists or recommendations of what to watch in streaming services, it is in the strategy of the machine in sports, in mobile processors, such as Huawei's Kirin 980, and even in the automated responses suggested when you write an email.

And there's still a lot to work with and the potential to take off in the future. Google Duplex, artificial intelligence that talks on the phone and plans to consult or reserve tables in restaurants, may become something far more fully in the conversation.

And there are also GANs (Generative Adversarial Networks) that are opposed to generating networks capable of generating content and creating photographs, videos, and sounds. Companies like Adobe will benefit significantly from this in the editing of applications like Photoshop. We've made many strides, but there's much work ahead of us.

This is the course of the evolution of artificial intelligence. This technology is already fantastic and essential for our everyday lives. Still, there's a lot to be done, and you can be part of this story. Udacity is the first Artificial Intelligence School in Brazil and has specialized courses to help you become an expert on the subject, extend your knowledge and develop a respectful business curriculum.

Various Styles Of ARTIFICIAL INTELLIGENCE Systems & Methods

Every artificial intelligence researcher has his way of understanding the challenges and opportunities in the field.

Broadly speaking, they fall into two distinct approaches: symbolic AI and connecting AI.

In symbolic artificial intelligence, processes affect transformations using symbols, letters, numbers, or terms. They thus simulate the abstract reasoning behind the languages in which human beings interact.

Connecting AI, on the other hand, is inspired by the functioning of our neurons. Simulate, thus, the mechanisms of the human brain.

An example of the technology of the connectionist approach is deep learning, the ability of the computer to acquire deep learning, the imitation of the neural network of the brain.

Some also talk of a third approach, evolutionary AI, which uses algorithms inspired by natural evolution.

That is, the simulation of concepts such as climate, phenotype, genotype, perpetuation, selection, and death in artificial environments made it possible for artificial intelligence to invade our lives in the decades to come.

From then on, the advancement of AI began to progress along with the evolution of computers.

CHAPTER 4
HOW DOES ARTIFICIAL INTELLIGENCE WORK?

As the name suggests, AI aims to simulate a particular human characteristic: intellect. It focuses on the creation of systems that can perfectly replicate human reasoning. Rather than following lines of code, AI aims to build machines that can adapt, learn and perform tasks as human beings.

However, the simulation of the conditions of the human mind proved to be a much more complicated task than had been expected at the beginning of his studies. This is primarily due to the complexity of understanding and functioning of all the biological processes taking place in the human brain.

Artificial intelligence is also working through systems that require far more than is feasible in our day-to-day interactions. Codes and programming work by mathematical functions.

In general, the concept provides a function in which another value occurs when a certain value is added. It is important to note that these values are not arbitrary but have a sense and, thus, a function. Computer codes are therefore not random, each of which is responsible for the function of the device.

In this way, AI refers to a computer with the ability to process a large amount of data by innumerable codes. The way machines analyze and interpret data will rely a lot on their intent and method.

There is a broad range of technology-focused on artificial intelligence. There are many codes, data, and information accumulated over the decades of field research. This makes the process of teaching and learning to be infinitely superior to what can be expected.

AI is divided into two main types: Machine Learning and Deep Learning. We'll see their features and distinctions below.

Learning Machines

Machine Learning is one of the main branches of AI, responsible for many of its implementations in the mainstream sense and businesses. It is a more straightforward approach to implementation and requires, as we have already said, preparation and learning.

However, we can classify Machine Learning into three forms of learning: supervised, unsupervised, and reinforced.

1. Supervised

The supervised form requires the active involvement of human beings to demonstrate the way to the systems. In other words, the programmer must transfer the database to the algorithm and a list of the results associated with that entry. The AI can find unique patterns and create its own way to get from the entrances to the respective exits.

It is then possible to simply input new knowledge. The algorithm will be able to answer this question based on what it has already studied. This type of modeling is also known as predictive, as the program would need to make an active prediction of potential outcomes.

To make this more practical: in an example that uses AI to classify which bank users can receive an increase in the credit card cap. The system receives thousands of customer data as input and training bases, with payment characteristics, history, income data, jobs, among other issues.

In the same way, it will obtain a base of only previous exits, i.e., right results on the risk of granting a cap or not. This is part of the testing and monitoring. Upon knowing this, the algorithm will be able to formulate its approach. It will evaluate the customer's new case to determine whether or not the bank can issue a credit increase.

We have two primary forms of supervised learning: classification and regression. The classification attempts to evaluate the data in order to categorize the component as X and the other as not X. For example, there are two categories in the credit example: you must receive the increase or not receive it.

In regression, the goal is to estimate a value in a certain way. So we're talking about projecting benefit in the realm of a campaign with such tactics, for example. Or a loss in real life with the realization of some danger.

However, this instruction should not require unsupervised or descriptive learning with potential outcomes because the programmer doesn't have any output knowledge. The software also must define the applicable standards and organize the data to know how to find solutions.

2. Unsupervised

Unsupervised learning is categorized into several other types: association, classification, outlier identification, and summarization, in particular. The association aims to identify trends and data associations in databases, such as finding that when users buy X, they appear to buy Y at the same session. This is done with statistical analysis. The classification, in turn, attempts to assign users from one base to another in various categories.

Detection of outliers is used to identify odd trends in data, such as any details that vary from what is conventional. On the other hand, summarization includes the development of summaries of knowledge of what is most relevant in a data collection.

3. Reinforcement

We also have reinforcement learning, which is based on a type of training based on scores and rewards. If the algorithm gets it right, it's rewarded. If it misses, it's going to lose points. Based on these points, it is possible to continue with the instructions.

Strengthening learning, in fact, is manifested in programs that try to learn particular human behavior, such as robots with artificial intelligence that try to move or systems that learn to play games like chess.

Algorithms

There are many standard algorithms about the workings of artificial intelligence. In this post, two of them will be addressed: the Naive-Bayes and the Decision Trees. Naive is statistically based: the method analyzes the data, understands its associations, and produces probabilistic weights for the output choices. Then the alternative is most likely to become a recommendation.

In tree decisions, what happens is the following: calculations are made to determine the nodes and branches of each point in the tree. From there, the device analyzes the conditions. It descends the tree in search of a response to a collection of input data. For example: "If the salary is > 10,000, then X; if the salary is <10,000, then examine the history node."

The Deep Learning

On the other hand, we have a more profound and more complex method commonly used to improve learning: Deep Learning (DL). This requires more data than Machine Learning and outputs results more realistically. One of the critical reasons for this is that most Deep Learning algorithms include neural networks.

Neural networks are systems that attempt to replicate the activity of human neurons for machine learning. As a result, there are multiple nodes in the network, and each of these nodes contributes to the solution of the problem. They are structured in many layers. The more layers, the higher the efficiency of the device.

Each node is trained in the database, making previous assessments and initial conclusions. From their findings, they become experts on a certain factor, which is precisely what they could better understand in this initial study. With this, each layer specializes in some dimension of the problem analyzed, which produces a consistent result at the end of the analysis of all of them. Each layer completes everything and forwards the information to the next layer.

For example: in image processing, a common form of Deep Learning application, one layer is responsible for recognizing shapes, while the other is responsible for detecting colors. As a result, the issue is going through some others. Finally, there is a layer at the end that can finally tell what the picture is about. This is the collaborative work of these specialist nodes.

Since more data is required, Deep Learning also requires more computing power, which requires more from the GPU. So it's perfect for some kind of more complicated problems, just not for all. As we have already said, cloud computing is critical to provide the structural basis for this type of algorithm to function correctly.

Machine Learning and Deep Learning's fundamental distinction is that there is a particular training stage in the first and an already knowledgeable algorithm in the second. In Deep Learning, the two phases are only one, which means that the program delivers faster results. It is advantageous to have this agility in cases where real-time analysis is needed.

CHAPTER 5

UNDERSTANDING ARTIFICIAL INTELLIGENCE

Artificial Intelligence can often seem like magic: many scientists and engineers combine electronics, computation, and robotics to create something that can perform tasks and interpret the environment much like a human being. Only over 50 years ago, that was pure science fiction. Nowadays, we're moving closer and closer to building an almost human intellect.

But this isn't magic: it's science. It is the product of years of research in computer science, electronics, mechatronics, and even psychology, always striving to develop prototypes to get closer and closer to the electronic version of the human brain.

Although the specifics of the most recent and robust implementations include very advanced concepts, the basic operation of Artificial Intelligence is straightforward to understand and essentially consists of three parts:

1. Get the data

An algorithm can only be called Artificial Intelligence if it has the ability to analyze and adjust its environment. And it requires sensors to analyze the environment. Sensors are electronic instruments capable of collecting data on the environment. Each sensor is modified to acquire a form of data. For example, there are sensors for motion, distance, location (such as GPS), color, image (i.e., cameras), among other forms.

The sensors shall be responsible for obtaining and transmitting this data to the processing center of the system in digital and/or analog form, which shall interpret it as being programmed.

2. The decision-making phase in the area of artificial intelligence

Decision-making is the most crucial aspect of this. It is its consistency that determines the "intelligent" nature of artificial intelligence. Developing this is the most time-consuming and crucial part of AI development.

The decision-making method is nothing more than a very complex algorithm that aims, at all times, to achieve the pre-determined objective of the AI while evaluating the environment (from the data of the sensors) to know what to do and what not to achieve your target.

Thus, the algorithm needs to be robust enough to always know what to do, based on the characteristics of the environment and the obstacles it encounters. This is something more accessible or more complicated, depending on the type of sensor used.

If only distance sensors are used, it is much easier: it is a matter of using the distance from the object to the robot to decide how to solve it. That is why they are commonly used, for example, in robots made to participate in the Brazilian Robotics Olympiad, since they have obstacles to conquer. Still, they are just rectangular and uniform objects.

If, on the other hand, cameras are used, it is essential to use computer vision algorithms to identify potential obstacles and to estimate the distance between them. These algorithms are much more complex and require more computing power on the part of the AI processor.

Nowadays, instead of programming AI, it is becoming more popular to use a machine-learning algorithm to "teach" artificial intelligence to pursue the target and address obstacles. Something that dramatically facilitates their development, although it requires ample storage space for computing power to work.

3. Acting on the conclusions

But, of course, all this effort to collect data, research, and decision-making would be in vain if they weren't used for anything. There are actuators for this: mechanical devices built to work in the environment. There are several simpler ones, such as motors, pumps, pistons, and solenoids. Still, there are also more complicated ones, typically due to the combination of many simpler parts, such as robotic arms and legs.

After artificial intelligence passes through the entire decision-making process, it comes to a conclusion that can take the form of action. If so, the appropriate algorithm will run. This algorithm will use the actuators available in a predetermined series to achieve the desired result. Whether this result is consistent with the current state of the environment and the goal to be accomplished would depend on the decision-making process, the configuration of the sensors, the output algorithm, among several other factors.

CHAPTER 6
CLASSIFICATION OF ARTIFICIAL INTELLIGENCE STYLES

The main goal of research on the advancement of artificial intelligence is to ensure that computers or technical systems have the capabilities that humans have. The degree to which gadgets can accomplish this aim is used to decide what kind of artificial intelligence they are.

Suppose one type of intelligence manages to stand out in terms of performance levels and is very similar to the performance of a human being. In that case, it is considered to be a more evolved type of intelligence. In contrast, intelligence that does not produce a result that stands out from the rest is considered to be less evolved.

Artificial Intelligence Can Be Graded In Two Ways

The first is the capacity of the computer to 'think' and even 'feel' as a human. The other classification is widely used in technology expression, including narrow or poor AI, general AI, and artificial superintelligence.

Following the first definition, there are four types of artificial intelligence or systems based on artificial intelligence: Reactive, Limited Memory, Theory of Mind, and Self-awareness. Next, we're going to tell you what each of them consists of.

Reactive Machinery

The most basic form of Artificial Intelligence system is reactive machines. This means that they cannot form memories or use past experiences to affect decisions taken in the present. They can only respond to current conditions, so they are reactive.

The current form of a reactive system is Deep Blue, an IBM chess-playing supercomputer in the mid-1980s.

Deep Blue was created to play chess against a human opponent with the goal of beating the competitor. It was equipped with the ability to recognize the chessboard and its parts while knowing the roles of the pieces. Deep Blue could make predictions about the moves it should make and the moves that its opponent could make, thereby having a more extraordinary ability to anticipate, pick, and win. In a series of matches played between 1996 and 1997, Deep Blue beat Russian chess grandmaster Gary Kasparov, becoming the first computer program to defeat a human opponent.

Deep Blue's unique ability to play chess reliably and effectively underscore his reactive skill. Similarly, his reactive mind often suggests that he has no understanding of the past or the future. He only knows and behaves in the present-existing universe and its components. For convenience, reactive machines are programmed for here and now, but not before and after.

Reactive machines have no world concept and cannot work outside the basic tasks for which they are programmed. One of the features of reactive machines is that they will still behave the way they've been programmed no matter the time or location. There is no development with reactive machines, only regression in repetitive behavior and behaviors.

This is where things get futuristic and complicated, as we imagine from the moment we hear the words 'artificial intelligence.'

The first two forms of artificial intelligence are present in many devices and systems that we know today. Still, the two that remain are actually ideas or real works of art in progress.

Thousands of researchers are actively working to innovate and apply the principle of mind intelligence.

When this kind of artificial intelligence is reached, the robots will be able to comprehend the actors with whom they communicate by recognizing their desires, feelings, values, and mental processes. To achieve this ambitious aim, it is vital to master the field of artificial emotional intelligence and other disciplines.

Making the artificial intelligence system fully understood by humans, that we change our minds all the time and have a very dynamic mind shaped by thousands of variables, would undoubtedly be one of the biggest challenges for science. So far, it is clear that humans have not been successful.

Mind Theory

What constitutes the philosophy of mind is the capacity to make choices to the same degree as human beings but by utilizing computers. While several computers currently have human capabilities, such as voice assistants, none are completely capable of talking about human values. The human conversation has emotional potential or sounds and acts like an individual does in standard conversational conventions.

This future class of computer capabilities would require the awareness that humans have thoughts and feelings that affect behavioral performance and thus influence the reasoning process of a "theory of mind" machine. Social interaction is a crucial facet of human interaction so that mental machine theory is observable. AI systems that control machines now need to recognize, maintain, and recall emotional development and actions while knowing how to respond.

Based on this, the mental computer hypothesis will have to be able to use knowledge taken from individuals and adapt it to their learning centers in order to know how to interact and deal with various circumstances. Mind theory is a very advanced type of proposed Artificial Intelligence that would require machines to fully identify the rapid changes in human emotional and behavioral habits and also to realize that human behavior is fluid, so the theory of mental machines would have to be able to learn rapidly at any given time.

Any aspects of the theory of Artificial Intelligence actually exist or have existed in the recent past. Two notable examples are the robots Kismet and Sophia, developed in 2000 and 2016, respectively.

The Kismet was able to interpret human facial signals, feelings and to mimic the emotions of his face, which was structured with human facial features: eyes, lips, ears, eyebrows, and eyelids.

On the other side, Sophia is a humanoid robot. What separates it from previous robots is its physical similarity to human beings and its ability to see, image recognition, and react to interactions with appropriate facial expressions.

These two human-like robots are signs of moving towards a complete theory of the Artificial Intelligence systems of the mind that will materialize in the near future. While none of them has the potential to have an entire human conversation with a real person, the two robots have similar emotional capability aspects to their human counterparts, a step towards smooth assimilation into human society.

Self-Consciousness

Self-awareness is still a conceptual concept, but it is the final stage of artificial intelligence. As the name suggests, this will occur when a device or computer has the ability to be aware of its own presence.

A system of self-awareness must be able to recognize and evoke emotions for others with whom it communicates and at the same time have thoughts, emotions, needs, values, and even desires of its own.

This degree is the objective that artificial intelligence research aims to achieve, even though it means years or even centuries of continuous work and effort.

Can Artificial Intelligence Be Attained With Self-Awareness?

At present, we are at level three of the four types of Artificial Intelligence, so assuming that we might theoretically achieve the fourth level of AI does not seem like a far-fetched notion.

But for now, it's important to concentrate on the development of all aspects of Type Two and Type Three in AI. Speeding at all levels could be harmful to the future of Artificial Intelligence for decades to come.

Second Classification Of Artificial Intelligence

As we have already discussed, this classification is used rather than anything in the field of information technology. It consists of four forms of artificial intelligence:

Narrow Or Weak ARTIFICIAL INTELLIGENCE

Weak Artificial Intelligence focuses on designing systems that struggle to think and deliberately solve problems like humans. This means that a computer equipped with Weak AI could process data and deliver results without self-awareness in Strong Artificial Intelligence.

The Natural Language Processing that we saw earlier is part of the Weak Artificial Intelligence sector. In this case, computers use software and algorithms created for particular purposes, such as the simulation of a human conversation.

Currently, most of the advancements considered critical to the area have been made in the Weak Artificial Intelligence Circle, with no progress being made in the area of Strong AI.

If we go back to the first classification process, that's where reactive machines and limited memory machines will come in.

Strong Artificial Intelligence

Strong Artificial Intelligence requires the development of systems capable of reasoning and problem-solving. It is thus known as self-conscious.

Strong AI is the key subject of the dispute since it raises discussions already known as the principle of consciousness in computers.

It also raises ethical issues resulting from the existence of structures that are cognitively different from human beings.

Powerful Artificial Intelligence and the discussions surrounding it are frequently explored in science fiction: 'Me, Robot' and 'The Bicentennial Man,' by Isaac Asimov, and 'AI-Artificial Intelligence,' by Steven Spielberg are good examples.

GENERAL ARTIFICIAL INTELLIGENCE

It refers to the ability of machines to think, read, interpret, understand and behave like human beings. It is surprising to imagine that systems with this kind of artificial intelligence will make correlations and generalizations with very little training time.

Examples include image processing machines, handwriting and speech recognition, natural language processing, and predictive learning utilizing Big Data.

Artificial Superintelligence

This level of intelligence will be a peak of intelligence types, equivalent to everything on planet Earth. Basically, aside from matching the human brain's multi-faceted capacities, it will be superior in all its behaviors and decisions. This, due to the infinite memory, data processing, and interpretation, can be decided in the most correct way possible.

Is Robotics The Same Thing As Artificial Intelligence?

No, no. Some people associate artificial intelligence with robotics, even though they are separate terms. Robotics is a technology division that deals with robots. It includes the design, development, and programming of physical robots, with only a portion of them involving artificial intelligence.

Robots are programmable devices capable of carrying out a series of actions independently or semi-autonomously. In general terms, robots are characterized by communicating with the physical world through sensors and actuators; they are programmable, autonomous, or semi-autonomous. However, there is no complete consensus on the concept of a robot. Some claim that a robot needs to be able to think and make decisions (which, in this case, suggests that it has some level of artificial intelligence).

Even when AI is used to control robots, algorithms are just part of a more extensive robotic system, including sensors, actuators, and non-AI programming.

In conclusion, artificially intelligent robots are a bridge between robotics and AI. Still, many robots do not need artificial intelligence, such as those that perform repetitive motions and have been around in factories for a long time.

CHAPTER 7
INTRODUCTION TO MACHINE LEARNING

In the last two decades, Machine Learning has become one of the foundations of information technology and, as a result, a key but generally secret part of our lives. With the rising amount of data available, there is good reason to believe that intelligent data analysis would become increasingly common as a critical ingredient for technological advancement.

This section aims to provide the reader with an overview of the broad range of applications that have a machine learning problem in their hearts and to introduce the reader to such an important subject, and to make users aware that Artificial Intelligence uses machine learning, deep learning and other techniques to solve real problems, so that AI does not exist without Machine Learning. Machine learning will happen without AI.

If more data become available thus, machine learning models will make better choices. As a result, AI will be improved.

In addition to providing basic knowledge of machine learning, we will also present some of its critical applications and discuss some of the basic statistics and probability theory tools. They form a vocabulary in which many machine learning problems need to be formulated to be amenable. It's a solution.

The topic of machine learning can be understood through a variety of approaches. We'll start with its conceptualization and its key applications.

CHAPTER 8
WHAT IS MACHINE LEARNING

Machine Learning, the original term in English, or automatic learning, as it is often called, is a sub-field of computer science. It has evolved from the study of pattern recognition and the theory of computational learning in artificial intelligence.

According to Arthur Samuel (1959), machine learning is "a field of research that gives computers the ability to learn without being specifically programmed." In addition, it discusses the design of algorithms that can learn from their errors and make predictions about data from two learning approaches: supervised, unsupervised, and reinforced. This helps you to make accurate and repeatable decisions and outcomes.

Such algorithms may make predictions from samples or make decisions based solely on data, without any kind of programming. Although similar in some respects to computational statistics, which make assumptions about using computers, machine learning is used in computational tasks where the design and programming of explicit algorithms are impractical.

Examples of applications include natural language processing, SPAM filtering, speech and handwriting recognition, computer vision, medical diagnosis, search engines, among others.

Applications for Machine Learning

Most readers of this blog are familiar with the web page ranking idea that Google has popularized. This is the method of submitting a query to the search engine, which then identifies the appropriate web pages for the query and returns them in their order of relevance.

In order to accomplish this purpose, the search engine must "know" which pages are important and the pages conform to the query. This information can be obtained from various sources: through the connection structure of the web pages, their content, the frequency with which users can follow the links indicated in the query, or through examples of queries in conjunction with manually categorized web pages.

More and more machine learning, rather than guesswork, is used to automate the process of making a successful search engine, such as Google. Collaborative filtering, a method used by the recommendation systems, is an application similar to this.

The Recommendation System incorporates statistical techniques for selecting customized objects based on the needs of consumers and on the context in which they are inserted. Online retailers, such as Amazon, or streaming services, such as Netflix, use this mechanism to encourage users to purchase additional items (or watch more movies).

The issue with the recommendation systems is very close to the rating of the web page. As before, we're trying to get a sorted list. The key difference is that there is no clear question. Instead, we can only use user activity to forecast potential viewing and purchase behaviors.

The preliminary information, in this case, is the decisions taken by similar users, hence the shared nature of the process. It is obviously advantageous to provide an automated system to solve this issue, avoiding guesswork and wasting time.

Another example of machine learning is the automated translation of documents. To solve this problem, we should try to fully understand the text before translating it, using a collection of selected rules developed by a computational linguist well versed in the two languages that we would like to translate. However, this will be a very challenging problem, as the text is not always grammatically correct. The meaning used can contribute to a lack of understanding.

Instead, we might only use examples of related translated documents. These documents should be used so that the computer can learn the translation between the two languages. In other words, we might use translation examples to learn how to translate. This machine learning approach has proved popular and is widely used, as the Internet itself is a great database.

Many security systems, such as access controls, use facial recognition as one of their components. That is, provided a picture (or video) of an individual. They can be recognized. In other words, the machine needs to distinguish faces from a wide range of categories (João, Camila, Felipe, ...) or decide that this is an unknown face.

The same problem, but conceptually very different, is that of verification. Your goal is to see if the person in question is whom they claim to be. Note that unlike before, this is a matter of yes or no. In order to cope with various lighting conditions, facial expressions, whether a person wears glasses, hairstyles, etc., it is desirable to have a device that learns which characteristics are relevant to the identification of a person.

Conclusion

Artificial intelligence is a technology that has the ability to make a variety of processes more effective, thereby helping people and improving their standard of living. However, machine learning is necessary if it is to be applied appropriately.

CHAPTER 9
THE FUTURE OF MACHINE LEARNING

In the current economic circumstances, any company is essentially a data business. Forrester Consulting conducted a study that found that over ninety-eight percent of the organizations felt that analytics are very significant in driving business strategy. Still, less than forty percent utilized additional and artificial intelligence or machine learning. For companies, there is a prominent machine learning opportunity to harness the power of their data and significant potential for greater gains and reduce costs.

Instead of doing a whole new analysis, a company would instead use predictive analysis or complex pattern recognition to help itself move up the business intelligence (BI) maturity curve. Bring in more nuanced decision-making processes and a desire to objectively incorporate descriptive analysis in order to address the apparent current trend towards a continued lack of futurism. At least as far back as 50 years ago, technological innovation and new product introductions have always been happening rapidly. Still, many businesses are starting to look at the technology afresh.

Often, real-time machine learning (and/is driven by) statistical analysis adds another dimension to business intelligence. While the legacy models continue to provide vital information to policymakers, real-makers put it at the fingertips of the front-line staff, who can make decisions in real-time to increase their performance.

Artificial intelligence technology subsumes the entire algorithms that are trained on substantial quantities of data to use on a more minor data set of attributes to examine and make predictions and suggest new sets of options to users. Previous simulations of the model can become outdated. They can be enhanced if the model is exposed to new data if it doesn't have human interference. This means that the model is less likely to generate erroneous results if used several times and more likely to learn.

In the long term, this furthers the "smarts" in all these directions, making systems "smarter" and more accurate and making them capable of revealing what they had once shielded from view, being able to decipher more extended patterns, historical relationships, and fostering the growth of new insights such as a, namely about market conditions, and oil production. There is a significant focus on using machine learning with big data because it allows businesses to reach greater analytical depth levels and include new functionalities such as IoT (Internet of Things) analyses.

Using powerful technologies like machine learning is nice for analytics at the moment. Many commercial and open-source machine learning solutions are available, and an extensive ecosystem of free and open-source models. Your organization may be already using this strategy, C. on an in email spam filters. Today, when you're collecting a massive amount of data and using new and more advanced technologies like machine learning and analytics, you can move quicker and stay ahead of the competition.

The ability to harness the massive amounts of data now available to produce insightful results for everything from customer target marketing to traffic forecasting

Analytics that are growing in prevalence is attributable to the fact that analytics provides tremendous market value across numerous industries due to machine learning's advancement. There are cases where a large quantity of historical and/forecasted data must be recalibrated regularly, where you will benefit from machine learning.

Providing suggestions for hundreds of products like books, movies, clothes, and thousands of other categories is a commonly used machine learning technique. Not only that, but there are various other benefits as well.

Dramatically improved inventory management can be enabled by RFID (Radio Frequency Identification) and machine learning in retail via technology. The objective is to provide a quick review of the role of the issues as much as it is to decide how close the inventory is to the inventory. In this case, by applying machine learning, the knowledge that's currently available can also be used to enhance product positioning and to influence consumer behavior. Suppose this example is changed, for example. In that case, the system could view items that are doing well in the store where the physical finds them and organizes the products as a priority search. He could set up new systems to make the store more accessible.

Companies that incorporate a large amount of language will learn about their brand and goods. By combining machine learning and social media, they can identify people on social media by searching for these items. The program often identifies secret trends within a user's body language that reveal their interest or dissatisfaction with a product.

Technology has also taken a primary role in the deployment of sensors. Also, for self-driving cars, the vehicles must have data from multiple sensors input devices or other sensors combined in real-time to avoid situations with conflicting information.

Machine learning helps determine the probability that a location's suitability for wind or solar power generation.

Some of the machine learning algorithms that we can teach in addition to these are mentioned below. Based on past experience, it is a sound technique that is yielding excellent results.

An Easy To See And Well-Defined Competitive Advantage

machine learning give businesses an edge in solving challenges and finding insights because it helps them to complete their tasks and research to be done faster. The script has particular advantages in generating value in the following three scenarios:

The solution to a dilemma is not fixed. There is always new work to be done on the internet and offline monitoring a brand's reputation. A significant fact to observe concerning individual channels is that new ones are being built. When these kinds of changes cause much uncertainty, and each time they do, they push marketers to test using the rules-based methodology. They inadvertently increase the risk of achieving the wrong results machine learning models can be characterized as needing time to acquire and update their own representation, provide accurate representations, and free up resources for use in other models

It depends on the situation: in this case, a different solution might be employed. The cases have different origins, as a patient's personal or family background, age, lifestyle, and preferences regarding some medications. Their allergy history or sensitivity to others affects how they respond to care. learns to take into account the individual background and circumstances associated with each patient to provide personalized care while also reducing the consumption of health services

At the end of the day, the answer is outside of human capability: we are able to see: the names of loved ones, discern objects, and recognize them, but not explain why. What's the problem? There are so many variables. Trying out several different factors (expressions, volumes, intonations, utterances, sounds, recordings, accents, and dialects) to recognize and classify different voices in this form of voice analysis will allocate them to individual groups and define these variables as well. She was listening to the drum, the five-thousand-year-old pitch that, which, when you close your eyes and hold your hands close to your ears, sounds very new.

A computer that generates competitive advantage by making new decisions without the use of humans (theoretically speaking), that is, without having to be directly told to do so by human decision-makers the increasing the versatility of many others, such as (in medicine, for example) the field of cancer detection, production, and travel (in this case) (with sound as an additional signal for driving safety).

Better Than Anything Else We Have Seen Before

When machine learning is compared to other methods, it tends to give some advantages to IT professionals, companies, various ones to the data scientists, and some to the organizations, respectively.

What machine learning excels within new data is its flexibility and agility. The benefit of rule-based systems becomes especially important in static situations. Still, in dynamic environments, machine learning becomes particularly beneficial when data is constantly being updated. This is because it must not be configured or augmented continuously to obtain the desired results. It helps to shorten the amount of time needed to implement the program and cuts down on significant revisions.

The staff costs for machine-related analyses usually are lower than those needed for traditional algorithms. The firm at the beginning should employ experts such as those working in probability and statistics, along with machine learning algorithms and AI training methods that can provide the skills needed to complete the job. But when machine learning is deployed, the ability to adapt to predictive models could be left to the model's own devices, thereby reducing the number required to achieve model accuracy and reliability.

The ability to expand quickly has a bonus since it can be done without any physical or software changes. These learning algorithms are better at scale because they are designed to work in parallel. This means they can scale more rapidly, which eventually yields a faster answer to business problems. Systems that require human intervention are challenging to construct and manage as well. A significant advantage of machine learning is that it reduces the amount of reliance on people's ability to make decisions.

Finally, machine learning implementations can be less expensive than advanced research of the vast majority of the time. There are several, but not all, machine learning approaches that can be applied to multiple machines instead of a single high-end platform computer.

At the heart of machine learning, there are two fundamental questions that machine learners ask: 1. What kind of examples do I get? and 2. What kind of results will these examples teach me?

With progress in the use of machine learning, finding a business issue becomes more accessible because the technologies all have a straightforward, quantifiable value for the business. When an effective project is located, organizations must appoint experts and advise them on the processes of "thinking" and "instructions" or actions for the programs to carry out the required functions.

Based on its own experience and the machine receives samples of the user's inputs and must establish rules of behavior, previous customer data will improve proposal significance. Still, major brand recommendation systems rely on supervised learning.

Supervised learning: The device is typically supplied with a lot of labeled data (the "correct" answer") but less with neutral or general-purpose data. These supervised learning models have the same training purposes as their unsupervised models. Still, they are cheaper because of the lower cost. New data is also an excellent example of a category that should be focused on whether the input information is expected to change, such as trade or social media, or, over time.

Unsupervised learning: This is when the machine searches the data for structures and patterns without having prior expectations. In contrast, in this mode, products placed in-store or in this category cause other trends to be seen, such as out-of-of-store purchasing activity, which could yield changes in placement or advertisement ideas.

Instead of being set to one constant value to modify behavior as in classical learning, the system is allowed to perform, given a task to do, and then given reinforcement by providing "tickets" and "with a variable scheme to determine varying rewards and punishments. This recognition technique has been employed successfully in factories for things such as robots, for good or for bad, for whatever it is worth if you consider.

Deep Learning: Directed Intelligence

I've read about it in other ways than some papers that have spoken about artificial neural networks. Still, there seems to be no way they can create "superintelligences" bits of intelligence that can match the brain. Human intelligence incorporates both language and cultural competence and complex mathematical ability and uses visual cognition, abstract and creative processes. So, on the whole, the average person's brain isn't better suited to certain facets of cognitive function, such as concentration and focus, than others. However, we can make our computers even more versatile by putting them in the hands of our professionals.

Recent advances in artificial intelligence had a monumental impact on people. It helped a Go-playing program hide within the background of the strongest players, allowing it to beat the world champion in all five games easily. Many board games are still part of daily Asian culture in countries like China and the Philippines, where they originated more than 2,500 years later. Though it does not follow traditional Western chess rules, this game has a broader playing area (that is, it's not highly compact like western chess) and a less predictable final outcome (compared to chess).

Most people believe that the number of potential game configurations well exceeds the number of atoms globally, even though this is clearly not true. However, existing methods to date have only been able to cope with this complexity have been able to detect it is if they are better than that of human brains and, but it is only a matter of time before algorithms are established that can detect.

Except for the most uncomplicated initiatives, commercially applicable machine learning applications, an organization's efficacy would be dependent on mastering these fundamentals.

CHAPTER 10
DEEP LEARNING

Deep learning (or deep learning) is a machine learning technique that teaches computers to do what is normal to humans: learn by example. It is the central technology behind driverless cars, for example, that allows vehicles to recognize a "stop" sign or to distinguish a pedestrian from a street lamp. It is also essential for voice control on devices such as phones, tablets, TVs, and hands-free speakers. Deep learning has received a lot of publicity lately- and with good reason: it is capable of delivering previously unthinkable results.

In the field of deep learning, a computer model learns to perform classification tasks directly from images, text, or sound. Deep learning models can provide cutting-edge precision, often exceeding human-level efficiency. Models are trained using a comprehensive collection of labeled data and neural network architectures that include several layers.

How Does Deep Learning Work?

Deep learning is a function of artificial intelligence (AI) that mimics human brain function in data processing and sets standards for use in decision-making. It is a branch of machine learning in artificial intelligence with neural networks capable of learning from unstructured or unlabeled data without human supervision.

The aim is to solve problems and help detect fraud or money laundering, among other functions. Deep learning has developed alongside the digital age, which has led to a data explosion in all types and regions of the world. These data, known simply as big data, are derived from sources such as social media, Internet search engines, e-commerce websites, and online cinemas, among others. This large amount of data is readily available and can be shared via fintech applications, such as cloud computing.

However, the data, which is typically unstructured, is so vast that it can take decades for humans to comprehend and extract the relevant information. Companies understand the enormous opportunity that can arise from disclosing this wealth of knowledge and are gradually adapting to automated support AI systems. Deep learning uncovers vast volumes of unstructured data that humans could understand and process for decades to come.

Deep Learning And Automated Learning (Machine Learning)

One of the most popular AI techniques used to process big data is machine learning. This self-adapting algorithm increasingly obtains better analysis and patterns from experience or from newly added data.

For example, suppose a digital payment company wants to detect the existence or potential of fraud in its system. In that case, it could use machine learning tools for this purpose. The computer algorithm embedded in the computer model can process all transactions that take place on the digital network, detect patterns in the data set, and point out any irregularities found by the pattern.

Deep learning is a subset of machine learning that uses a hierarchical level of artificial neural networks with many hidden layers to perform machine learning. Artificial neural networks are constructed like a human brain, with "nodes" of neurons linked together, creating something close to a web. Although conventional programs produce linear data processing, the hierarchical function of deep learning systems allows machines to process data with a non-linear approach.

A conventional approach to detecting fraud or money laundering could rely on the number of transactions that occur. Simultaneously, a non-linear deep learning technique would involve time, geographical location, IP address, the type of retailer, and any other resource that might point to fraud in a number of layers. The first layer of the neural network processes raw data input, such as the transaction value. It transfers it as output to the next layer. The second layer processes and transmits the information from the previous layer, including additional information, such as the IP address of the user.

The next layer takes the information from the second layer. It adds raw data, such as geographical location, making the machine pattern even better. This continues at all stages of the neural network.

How Deep Learning Works

Using the fraud detection method described above with machine learning, an example of deep learning can be given. Suppose the machine learning algorithm has created a model with parameters built around the amount of money that the user sends or receives. In that case, the deep learning method will begin to compile data from the results offered by machine learning.

Each layer of the neural network builds on its previous layer with the addition of additional data, such as vendor, sender, consumer, social media case, credit score, IP address, and a host of other features that would take years to be computed by a human. Deep learning algorithms are trained not only to establish patterns for all transactions but also to know when a pattern suggests the need for a fraudulent investigation. The final layer transmits a signal to an analyst who can freeze the user's account until all pending inquiries have been completed.

Deep learning is used in a variety of different tasks for all fields and sectors. Commercial applications that use image recognition, open-source networks with user recommendation applications, and medical research tools that investigate the possibility of reusing medicines for new diseases are examples of incorporating deep learning.

A Brief History Of Deep Learning

Machine learning is thought to have emerged in the 1950s, when Alan Turing, a British mathematician, proposed his artificially intelligent machine learning. Arthur Samuel wrote the first application in machine learning. Decades afterward, numerous machine learning methods have gone in and out of fashion.

Machine learning researchers largely overlooked neural networks. They were plagued by the issue of "local minimums," in which weightings wrongly seemed to indicate the least number of errors. However, some machine learning methods, such as computer vision and facial recognition, have progressed. A machine learning algorithm called Adaboost was created in 2001 to detect faces in an image in real-time.

However, the most important move towards the popularization of neural networks was the release of large volumes of data labeled with ImageNet, a collection of millions of labeled images from the Internet. The inefficient job of manually tagging images has been replaced by crowdsourcing, giving networks an almost limitless source of training materials.

Application Programming Interface For Deep Learning

Deep learning is present in apps, streaming platforms, social networking, and various services you use every day. For example,

Facebook recognizes and tags your friends when you upload a picture because of deep learning.

Digital assistants such as Siri, Cortana, Alexa, and Google Deep learning are also used for natural language processing and speech recognition. Skype turns spoken conversations into real-time. Many email platforms will detect spam even before it hits the inbox. PayPal introduced an in-depth learning method to avoid fraudulent payments. It's a long list!

Deep learning is still in its infancy but aims to change society in the coming decades. Autonomous cars are being tested worldwide; a complex layer of neural networks can be programmed to identify traffic lights and know when to change the speed.

Neural networks can learn and forecast anything from stock markets to weather conditions. Deep learning apps can also save lives as they develop the potential to develop evidence-based care plans for sick people and even help diagnose different forms of cancer early. The future is profound learning.

CHAPTER 11
THE FUTURE OF DEEP LEARNING

Many others can struggle to keep up with deep learning because of its difficulty. Anything new or different about it would probably make the work much more difficult. The trick is to be able to keep up with new technologies. It is beneficial to know the future that awaits the arrival of deep learning.

We'll first take a look at what deep learning is. For the most part, it is performed by AI or AI. The AI can self-teach and self-learn by being given free, neutral, unordered input. Instead, it can be "unstructured," "entirely dissevered," or free-form data and learns from this. Using artificial neural networks, it's known as deep learning and is gaining in complexity quickly. The newly invented science of artificial intelligence is able to go through social media, search engine data, search results, and eCommerce sites to find out what people want to know and give them crucial commercial knowledge.

As Deep learning advances, it grows in capability and applicability. It also develops in-depth, eventually providing more superb insights and inferences. The final product would be very clever. It will have all the data at once instead of making multiple calls to multiple websites. It concentrates on learning facts but can never be entirely understood since there is too much information for the human mind to process.

It makes sense that future generations of AI and deep learning will differ from those we have today. After all, it's growing increasingly, and it will soon become more advanced than what we know.

Deep Compression Is A Thing

Deep compression may minimize the amount of space that an app or program requires on laptops or phones. With apps and files increasing exponentially in size, there is a need to reduce the amount of space they take up. There are many options available for AI, but AI applications tend not to run on phones because of how much space they need, not to mention processing power.

In the near future, deep compression can be expected to become a thing. This will allow information to be compressed just like a JPEG. The end result would be a reduction of 550 MB to 10 MB, more or less. This will enable AI apps to operate on almost any computer.

Facial Recognition And Follow-Up

No one wants to think about it, but facial recognition is part of the world we're living in right now. It's only used in a couple of applications and has seen some pretty bad press lately, but it's growing. Just remember how Facebook lets you know that you could be shown in a picture so that you can tag it yourself. Some phones are also using facial recognition as a security feature.

All this is going to be bigger and better soon. You're definitely going to see it soon in shopping and probably in advertisements. Machines can quickly decide who's interested in what and then guide them to highly targeted advertising. It may also be possible to see advertisements aimed at you when out in public, as advertising cameras capture your face and personalize the marketing messages you see.

Predictions Making

With deep learning, it is possible to process vast quantities of data within such a short period of time that AI can make predictions quickly. There are weather forecasts, of course, that we depend on to decide what to wear every day, but that's much more than that.

Marketing and revenue forecasts are infinitely more helpful and offer businesses an objective. For example, suppose a particular product is expected to do well in the coming year. In that case, the company will be able to roll out products related to that product. There are several ways to use the details. Still, you want to make sure that you have reliable machine data to predict what could happen in the next few months.

Ethics Within ARTIFICIAL INTELLIGENCE

We've all heard of the three principles of robotics, but what about when it comes to ethics and AI? After all, computers will learn like humans at this stage, collecting data that even people can't calculate correctly. That puts quite a bit of power in the hands of the AI.

As artificial intelligence continues to become more intelligent, we are likely to see more legislation working directly on these issues. For example, new rules might be put in place to decide who is at fault if anything goes wrong because of the AI system. It would also be imperative for businesses to be honest about how they use the data obtained by those using their platforms. It is also likely that the government will ultimately get interested in avoiding ethical problems.

CHAPTER 12

ARTIFICIAL INTELLIGENCE BLENDING TO OTHER TECH

We've seen more and more combinations of technology. We are likely to see some changes in this field soon. E.g., AI is blended with IoT (Internet of Things), and Blockchain is already working on it.

Things like self-driving cars, route planning, and natural language processing are a few things that need technology to be merged with AI, and there will only be more of this in the future. There are precedents for this, and there will be more in the future.

The future of deep learning is fast approaching. We've already seen so many impressive improvements that you never know what's going to happen. We can only assume that.

Big Data

A variety of market disturbances characterizes the 2010 decade. We have Nubank, with credit cards, Banco Inter with a digital account that does not charge any fees, and AirBnB with hotel service. The prospect of changing the way things have always been done, getting away from the conventional, and providing the services that customers have always dreamed of, is made possible with all the technology available and open to all.

The development of new goods, more targeted ads, and better decision-making are taking place thanks to Big Data and knowledge transfer between various data sources.

Yet many people are asking themselves, "What is this big data?" As the amount and variety of data make up the power of Data Marketing, the use of the Big Data concept is becoming essential in our everyday lives. Therefore, in this section, we will clarify what Big Data is and all its possibilities for you to understand how promising this definition and its applications are in your everyday lives.

CHAPTER 13
WHAT IS BIG DATA?

Big Data is a term that describes the large volume of structured and unstructured data produced every second.

For many, the Big Data idea is something new. Even before any digital media and/or computing technology was available, data has already been developed (as shown in this timeline of the Win shuttle website). The difference is that today we're generating a lot more data with devices like mobile phones and TVs. Also, we have social media that mainly produce public information at all times. Today, the presence of interconnected vehicles, refrigerators, and wearable devices (wearable devices) is already a fact, creating even more data to be processed and converted into useful information.

The Big Data differential is precisely related to the potential and the ability to cross this data through multiple channels in order to gain fast and valuable insights. Consumer demand and increased competition in all industries compel us to innovate and to take this direction as a fundamental principle for a company.

That's why Big Data is so critical today. We are in a position to collect business insight from our customers, extracting what they think about everything you do. Dissatisfaction, happiness, wishes, needs, among others, can be captured on social media and cross-referred to the company's internal data, providing remarkable insights.

The essence of the idea is to create value for a business. The more data we have, the greater the processing effort required to produce information. Therefore, the speed of obtaining information is part of the success that Big Data will bring to your business.

If we talk about Big Data, we essentially have two forms of information structure: structured and unstructured data. Let's understand each other a little bit.

Let's understand each other a little bit.

Structured Data

Structured data are data with a particular structure, categories, clusters, and meanings, such as location, sales and customer profile details, contacts, among others.

Structured data is contained in databases because, in order to store any data, it is necessary to have very clearly specified where and information is to be stored. Software from companies such as ERP, CRM, financial systems, HR systems, and others has structured data.

Unstructured Data

Unstructured data is the most difficult to deal with since it does not even have a framework requiring human involvement in its preparation. We're talking about social media info, such as YouTube, Facebook, Instagram, news portals, etc. Many of the media we've listed deal with data in videos, photographs, text, and even audio, so the difficulty of managing this data is more significant.

Today, we can track social media by capturing public feedback and mentioning a specific keyword. That is, we can track what people think about your business or even the market in which you work in general. However, the most effective way to structure these data is by human intervention. It is necessary to carry out a prior review of what is being commented on and the meaning of that reference. We have a few forms of statements that may sound optimistic, but in fact, they are words of sarcasm, irony, and, most of the time, robots are unable to catch.

Also, it is essential to establish tags as if they were categories for what they say in a given context. A human being must do this type of work (for now) since it includes several specific aspects of each project.

The general question is, "If I find 20,000 comments, does a human being need to categorize, tag and structure these data?" It's exactly. For this purpose, we consider the difficulty of unstructured data to be more extraordinary, more labor-intensive, and time-consuming.

BIG DATA HISTORY AND CONCEPT

It might not sound like that, but the idea of big data is relatively old.

After all, it is not only today that a large amount of data is being handled by the systems.

If you think about it, recall when the British set up a computer to crack Nazi codes during the Second World War.

At that time, with the invention, thousands of messages had been decoded in a matter of seconds.

In other terms, big data has already been used.

It was, however, only in 1997 that the word was used for the first time.

However, it was officially broadcasted in 2005 with the release of an article by Roger Magoulas, who worked for O'Reilly Media.

Magoulas was also one of those responsible for developing the definition of Web 2.0.

What's The Value Of Big Data?

Big data isn't just a data volume tool.

It is, in effect, a tool for strategic analysis.

This is because it is possible to gain helpful information on different topics while gathering, arranging, and interpreting the data collected.

In businesses, for example, the mechanism allows market opportunities to be found.

Big data is so expressive that a large part of the investments of digital transformation organizations should be concentrated in 2021.

AVEVA survey, a company specializing in manufacturing and engineering applications, heard 1,240 executives from around the world.

The study found that Artificial Intelligence, Cybersecurity, and Engineering Design are the corporate scenario priorities for this year.

The key emphasis is the study of large data volumes. Artificial intelligence was reported by 75% of the respondents.

Then there's Augmented Reality (64 percent), Virtual or Mixed Reality (60 percent), and Big Data Processing (59 percent).

Big Data Best Practice

Big data enables many applications, depending on the company's performance, the sector, and the objectives.

There are, however, practices that are essential to any business.

Use your big data to:

- Better understand the market in which it operates and anticipate trends
- Know your target audience and propose appropriate solutions
- Optimize your processes to reduce unnecessary risks and procedures.

Challenges For Big Data

So far, we have talked about the benefits of big data and the possibilities of using the activity.

Now is the time to list the main challenges facing the area.

Perhaps the biggest one is the restructuring needed for implementation.

This is because, for big data to be carried out with excellence, there needs to be a substantial technological infrastructure to support data processing.

In this sense, due to the effort to be made, some resistance among employees is common.

After all, everyone must work together to review the old processes and, in turn, to create new ones.

Another obstacle that can hinder the execution of big data is the lack of qualified labor.

Since it is a relatively young occupation, it is not easy to find experts in the field.

On the other hand, it can be a promising opportunity for someone thinking of building a good career.

Forms of Big Data

Now that you know how the data is organized, I will show you how the three forms of data that cover Big Data are classified. They contain mixed data on text, audio, video, pictures, among others. Come on, come on:

Social data: essentially people-based data and types of information that decode actions. In other words, we will define profiles here to function in a more targeted manner. When we have data on how people search Google and what they post on social media in their hands, we can see how predictable people are.

Enterprise data: Company-generated data at all times (financial data, human resources, operations, etc.). Some ignore this data, but it may be necessary to measure team efficiency and identify bottlenecks.

Personal data or data of things: still new mainly here in Brazil, this data is provided by refrigerators, cars, TVs, and other devices that are connected to the internet and that talk to each other. It is called the Internet of Things or IoT, a topic that has been widely discussed in 2015 and 2016 and is expected to be a significant trend in the coming years, including 2017. It is now possible, for example, to access information from Waze or Google Maps to produce real-time traffic information and feed electronic panels around the region, making life simpler for drivers with up-to-date real-time traffic information.

Crossing the data of these three forms is what gives the generation of critical business knowledge. You need to be alert, however. In the same proportion as we have acquired several opportunities for change and assertiveness, it is possible to lose the available data in the sea.

CHAPTER 14
ANALYTICS OF BIG DATA

You've also understood a bit more about the whole system that conceptualizes Big Data. Now it's time to talk about the work that makes it possible to cross all data: Big Data Analytics.

With Big Data Analytics, we extract, organize, process, and understand structured and unstructured data. We're talking about nothing less than translating data into valuable knowledge for you and your business to move forward with more excellent decision-making stability.

We have seen a little above that we have three forms of data-social data, enterprise data, and personal data to be explored and played out in the context of the possibilities that data can offer us. Here are several examples of where we can get the data and then handle it, creating the insights that we've spoken about so much.

E-mails: e-mails can be a great source of data. Some applications and web resources e-mail data files in a structured way. This information can be provided as an attachment in Xls, pdf, or even in the body of the email. From them, we can build robots or e-mail integrations to search for and process these data in the best way possible and provide the necessary details.

Social media: social media, such as Facebook, Twitter, Instagram, and the blog, provide valuable data that can be collected and translated into facts. We can see what people say on social media about problems relevant to their business or the market itself. As we have seen, social networking data is unstructured, so it is crucial to arrange this data to have something minimally understandable.

Open data: More and more governments in various countries release data on health, finance, consumers, the environment, and many other issues. We can use this data to cross-reference internal data sources to gain strategic business knowledge and make previously impossible decisions due to a lack of resources.

Web systems: tools such as Google Analytics, RD Station, Facebook Advertising, Bing Ads, among others, are rich data sources, so the business has the most value. Information about clients, tourists, and business opportunities. The discovery of these sources has become a fundamental choice for any company.

Excel and Google Drive spreadsheets Sheets of distribution: Many organizations have spreadsheets distributed through servers, computers, and the cloud, as is the case with Google Drive. For example, we can take this data and cross it with the data from emails to produce the required information.

As you have seen, a large part of the resources is being used in our everyday lives. All you do creates the data you want us to explore.

We should benefit from all of this. Suppose anything we do produces data, and people are predictable. In that case, it means that the knowledge produced by our actions will help us better understand what we do and how we do it, doesn't it?

Did you know that a number of businesses are now using Big Data Analytics to help, profit, and develop their processes? To prove what we've discussed so far, here are some businesses that use Big Data and how they do it.

Examples of the Use of Big Data

We've already been through some big data implementations. But how about getting more examples of different uses for different purposes?

Social Media

Social networks are the ideal environment for the establishment of big data.

This is because they have a high volume of data, with a wide variety of the speed.

These networks are great for the marketing of goods and services.

And, with data analysis, communication can be more assertively driven.

Buying Habits

This example is commonly used in the retail sector.

After all, when identifying customer behavior, tactics should be aligned.

Suppose a particular group of customers always buy a form of a product. In that case, you can get ahead and send a direct mail, telling them that it is time to repeat the purchase or suggest similar products they might be interested in.

Human Resources

The area of HR is ancient. For example, the recruiting process has been going on for many years.

However, this has been changed. Big data is a significant contributor to this evolution.

Available applications include the opportunity to develop strategies for selecting curriculums according to specific tasks that the organization seeks in new employees.

Financial Area

Every financial planner's dream is to distribute capital efficiently.

That is, to distribute values that are relevant to the needs of the organization.

This becomes possible with big data.

In addition to helping with visualization, the tool helps to understand the cost of better targeting and control.

Search

Big data used to search people, commonly on sites like Google, leads to marketing research.

The predictive analysis provided by the tool is a positive point when it comes mainly to segmentation.

For example, it is possible to understand where the number of searches is concentrated.

How will small and medium-sized companies profit from big data?

If you think that only giants and business leaders can use big data, you might be shocked by the details below.

This is because small and medium-sized enterprises will also benefit from this activity.

The critical point, without a doubt, is to understand the actions of its customers better.

As a result, action can be taken to increase process effectiveness, reduce costs and recognize opportunities.

The secret of this method is to consider the importance of the data at your disposal.

For example, everything you know about your target base can be used to qualify the strategy, both in what you give them and how you do it.

Who is Using Big Data?

After all, if big data works for everybody, who is applying it and taking advantage of it?

We've got examples from various industries to present to you.

Banks

Big data has a range of applications from financial institutions.

Among them, we highlight the use of technology to help manage credit risks for consumers and deter fraud.

University Education

Managing student records and campus information, financial management, and enhancing academic study are some of the advantages that big data gives educational institutions.

GovernmentS

The government also uses big data to manage population data, especially the beneficiaries of programs such as Bolsa Familia in Brazil, a popular social welfare program of the Government.

Hospitals

Big data also revolutionized the world of medicine. And it's no different for health care services.

The implementation of the approach has led to the registration and management of patient details in their medical records, including examinations, consultations, and procedures.

Manufacturers

There are several big data success stories in the automotive sector.

Improving the quality of production is one of them.

Data analysis makes it possible to improve production processes, product quality, and improve final delivery.

Retail

In the retail sector, big data has collaborated, above all, with data on the consumer behavior of consumers.

Commercial institutions should also develop solutions to improve their relationship with their audiences further.

CHAPTER 15

WHAT IS THE RELATIONSHIP BETWEEN AI AND BIG DATA?

There is a complex and dependent relationship between Artificial Intelligence and Big Data, which is why many people confuse the terms.

But we can better understand this relationship by making an analogy. In the opinion of some experts, AI will be like a human brain. That is, it is capable of storing and processing the knowledge it receives from human experience (reading, travel, crisis situations, etc.), and, based on this processing, you can propose solutions on your own.

And Big Data, what will it be like? It can be said, more or less, about the experiences we have, that is, the data that are produced from these experiences.

Thus, we can conclude that there is an intersection between AI and Big Data. AI algorithms run in the Big Data environment and create successful communication between these two areas, which are different and complementary at the same time.

The importance of AI and Big Data to organizations

From what we have already seen, we can be sure of AI and Big Data's value for contemporary society, focusing on organizations.

These are innovations that can not only enhance processes and procedures but together, ensure a transformation in the various departments of an organization, such as:

• reduce costs through the implementation of AI-based technologies that can conduct services or operations instead of human resources, as well as reduce costs because they prevent human error;

• increase data efficiency;

CHAPTER 16
WHAT IS PREDICTIVE ANALYSIS?

The amount of data produced every day is ridiculous. In addition to the expansion of conventional means of communication such as radio, TV, and newspapers, there is an increase in broadband internet, smartphones (which are now used by more than half of the population), and IoT (the Internet of Things or the Internet of Things).

Predictive analysis happens when this collection of available data is used to predict business dynamics and optimize processes. Techniques such as cloud computing, machine learning, algorithms, and memory technology are used to this end.

Based on historic data, models are developed to forecast something new or different and thus enable decision-making to ensure business performance.

Its main capabilities are as follows:

- Failure to figure out trends;
- Reasonable anticipation of behavior;
- discern the needs of the customer;
- Failure to make decisions based on hard data;
- Enhancing market efficiency.

HOW DOES PREDICTIVE ANALYTICS WORK?

Predictive research has a lot to do with conventional statistical data diagnosis.

It is not by chance that most predictive models are regressors, i.e., equations generated from data analysis.

In this context, terms such as big data, machine learning, and artificial intelligence are examples.

It also acts as a model that helps you to predict patterns or address questions about established issues.

Predictive Analysis in Business

Have you ever wondered if your business could forecast the future? That would have been quite an advantage, would you agree? It would also be possible to predict consumers' needs and be even more accurate in creating and producing goods and services. What if I tell you that there is a method that can help? This is predictive research!

Logically, this instrument isn't a crystal ball. However, it is a solution that has been implemented by businesses from the most diverse segments to solve challenges and to innovate.

Predictive research provides perspectives that are capable of predicting potential scenarios. In this way, more proactive planning can be encouraged, and inconvenience caused by unsuccessful decisions can be avoided. Predictive analysis means that decision-makers get better outcomes and are still one step ahead of the competition.

The predictions are based on complex data collected from the company's own spreadsheets and databases. The practice of using data for decision-making has been used for a long time, either to assess market results or to understand past behavior that can reflect on your goals and objectives.

In order to use data for the benefit of business, businesses opt for software and systems that allow easy visualization. Some of them adopt more straightforward methods, such as Excel. Others prefer more complex systems such as Power BI. Irrespective of the option. It is essential to provide an assertive and adherent business system. Successful outcomes can be obtained from the observed data.

Do you want to know what predictive analytics is? Read on to see how it operates and what the advantages are.

How Does The Predictive Analysis System Affect Your Company?

There are many ways for a predictive platform to impact your business. Still, we can say that from there, your decision-making will be more assertive, and your strategy will be more applicable to your operating reality and the market.

The optimization of your supply chain is a great benefit that we will highlight. Predictive insights would allow for more efficient planning concerning the procurement of inputs, the number of goods to be produced per year, the adaptation of labor during times of high demand, the purchase or exchange of equipment, the flow of output, and many other possibilities.

Artificial Intelligence also helps to recognize trends of use, purchases, and customers that can be used by marketing and commercial teams while structuring strategies to attract or maintain consumers.

Predictive systems may be used to detect potential production losses or delays, factors that contribute to reduced quality and reduced sales. This technology can also be used to avoid production issues and to maximize its resources and goods.

How Important is it to Make Data-Based Decisions?

For some time now, managers from various departments have noticed that the technological level has promoted profound changes in how business is conducted. The mechanisms involved in strategic decisions, making solely instinctive choices, are among the novelties. In addition to the metrics, KPIs, and studies on which directions can be centered, predictive analysis has also emerged in recent years.

Integrated databases, such as CRM, are used to conduct the analysis. Multiple variables are considered to understand customer behavior, industry dynamics, and business optimization options. With the information resulting from this intensive investigation process, forecasts of more accurate scenarios are produced.

For example, suppose the manager knows in advance that seasonality may increase the number of keyword searches used in the supported connection campaign. In that case, the strategy's budget will be increased. Based on the data, this decision makes it possible for the campaign not to be limited to a specific period of time applicable to the company.

This is only one way to use predictive analysis to enhance the company's operationalization and strategy. Still, other strategies can be implemented if the team can forecast outcomes and make decisions in advance.

Through basing these recommendations on legitimate knowledge and actual evidence, the manager will maximize the resources available, coordinate the team's activities more efficiently, protect against unintended scenarios and create more promising strategies.

These advantages can be achieved by making business decisions on science, not just guessing based on guesswork. The more the specialist looks at the data and has access to a more in-depth review, the more he will be able to provide better outcomes, some of them already in the short term.

How Does Predictive Analytics Help to Make Decisions?

As we have said, it is not just the knowledge derived from the predictive analysis that can help to make more strategic decisions: it poses some critical differences concerning alternatives such as KPIs and studies. We'll highlight four of them below.

Estimates About The Future

The significant gain posed by this Big Data pillar relates to the prospect of forecasting potential scenarios instead of providing just fragmented data on the actions of the public in the past.

While data mining operates with history, the goal is based on the trends found, predicting which scenarios the organization will face in the future is possible. Thus, managers' decisions are not based solely on expectations and small chances of success but on probabilities, understanding which scenario the algorithm is most likely to suggest.

Possibility Of Identifying Trends

The novelty of the knowledge collected also stands out concerning the forecasting capability of the strategy. Predictive analysis is still underutilized in the Brazilian industry, which means that companies investing in a solution have real advantages over the competition.

By understanding the industry dynamics, the manager is in a position to forecast habits and improvements, to be able to guide expenditure and resources into solutions that still do not receive due attention from competitors. This innovation offers the brand an ability to be more important to the customer, as it knows their needs in advance.

Optimizing Marketing Resources

Targeting resources and budgeting are among the most essential tasks in marketing management, as making these decisions based solely on previous campaign success can be somewhat unpredictable.

Through predictive analysis, these concepts are more rigorous since the growth potential of each activity is recognized, preventing the budget from being redundant in one channel while the other operates with limitations. Resources are also better used, resulting in more reliable and effective performance.

Easy To Predict Behavior

Knowing consumer behavior is vital to having a successful company. Yet, being able to anticipate shifts, demands and opportunities is an even more significant difference, as it enables the customer's path to be increasingly optimized.

The customer relationship also shifts as innovations are implemented in this context, making forecasting a strategic advantage of great value for the manager.

Predictive analysis is a solution that will rapidly acquire space within the company's divisions, in particular marketing, as it deals with sensitive activities that attract and engage consumers. Managers who recognize early on the advantages of this investment would be better able to make proactive decisions and produce better results for the business.

CHAPTER 17
THE FUTURE OF ARTIFICIAL INTELLIGENCE

The Benefits Of Artificial Intelligence For Big Corporations

Artificial Intelligence (AI) will have a more significant effect on humanity than the Internet itself. With it, we allow businesses to be more effective.

This is projected by TOTVS Laboratories, an international research laboratory. And these impacts are already being felt as we meet virtual assistants, autonomous vehicles, drones transporting goods, and even medical diagnostic robots.

According to studies by Stanford University, by 2030, our whole day will be changed with Artificial Intelligence, from the way we go to work to the way we take care of our wellbeing. The study "Artificial Intelligence and Life in 2030" forecasts how smart technology can impact areas such as health, safety, entertainment, education, and transport.

The consequences for large corporations, however, are the ones that stand out the most. Research by Tata Consultancy Services (TCS), which specializes in IT consulting and services, found that businesses that generated the highest sales gains (average 16 percent increase) and reduced costs associated with Artificial Intelligence were those that invested five times more in technology.

Meanwhile, the businesses that spent less saw sales growth of just 5%.

According to the same survey, 84 percent of businesses consider the use of Artificial Intelligence to be "important" to productivity, while another 50 percent see it as "transforming." In other words, businesses already feel the effect of Artificial Intelligence. Below, we bring you some places that might benefit from AI development in the business world.

Job Market

One of the significant concerns about artificial intelligence on the part of human talent is the prospect of seeing robots and intelligent systems taking over their work.

In reality, this is what Artificial Intelligence offers: to bring more skilled jobs to businesses, to replace people not just in operational roles but also in decision-making processes.

However, Artificial Intelligence systems such as Deep Learning, Natural Language Processing, and Cognitive Computing would be responsible for opening up new work. One of them will be the data analyst needed to make sense of all the knowledge provided by intelligent systems.

According to the TCS report on the effect of Artificial Intelligence on jobs, the executives interviewed expect a net reduction of between 4% and 7% for each role until 2020. However, the companies with the largest sales and cost efficiency gains produced by AI see a demand for new jobs at least three times higher in each position by 2020. The reasoning is that Artificial Intelligence would build new employment and services that have not been possible in the past.

AI is now being used to automate such processes, increase productivity, help workers be more efficient, and spend more time on strategic business needs. Therefore, companies must devote themselves to the work of directing workers to undergo this period of transition, in which existing jobs will be lost, and new ones will be produced.

Customer Relationship

Artificial Intelligence is commonly used to enhance the relationship with the consumer. Technology solves issues more quickly and anticipates potential purchases. The idea of cognitive computing has revolutionized operation, as it can understand human language, including slang, colloquialism, and regionalism. Besides, it recognizes photos, explanations, and answers itself. Although it has no love, technology can detect irony and still understand if the individual is nervous because of the sound of the voice.

An example of the use of this technology is the Poupinha chatbot, a virtual assistant to Poupatempo. In addition to offering guidance on the services provided, it can arrange appointments for hundreds of users at any time in any of the 72 units of Poupatempo in the State of São Paulo. The service has led consumers to believe that their needs have been thoroughly understood and that the robot has successfully met the demands. Proof of this is that the chatbot has already received more than 50 thousand thanks messages from users, which is equal to 23 percent of calls made.

According to the Forrester Research survey, 57% of respondents indicated that one of the main reasons for using Artificial Intelligence is to enhance customer service, which indicates that businesses are interested in using technology for this purpose.

Sales And Marketing

The effect on sales and marketing results from the enhancement of customer service generated by Artificial Intelligence. If the relationship with the customer improves, revenue will also increase.

Almost a third (32%) of the businesses interviewed by the TCS report will have the greatest effect of Artificial Intelligence on revenue, marketing, or customer support by 2020. AI is seen as an essential method, e.g., through Machine Learning, to enhance customer service by automating the creation of analytical models.

Machine Learning (or Machine Learning) is an implementation of Artificial Intelligence in which the system learns how to behave on its own, based on the data collected. The software thus becomes capable of learning without being specifically programmed. Another survey conducted by the Accenture Institute for High Performance found that 40% of the businesses interviewed used Machine Learning to boost sales and marketing performance.

Services and products that provide convenience and practicality are critical for creating customer loyalty. Artificial Intelligence is an alternative that helps to personalize the service. According to a survey conducted by Salesforce, 88 percent of marketers consider customer loyalty and dedication to be the critical indicator of success in the marketing campaign, which confirms the importance of Artificial Intelligence in a company's sales performance.

Information Technology Security

IT defense is still the field that enjoys more Artificial Intelligence. According to the TCS report, today, the IT departments are the ones that most embrace Artificial Intelligence in companies: almost 7 in 10 (68 percent) interviewees use AI to identify and avoid threats and attacks to security systems, user security problems, and automation.

Machine learning and intelligent algorithms are starting to significantly detect known and unknown threats, making IT security professionals take a more proactive security stance. The advancement of cognitive systems has also led to the protection of organizations, as they have the potential to make accurate and stable data-based decisions. As a result, area managers learn to trust AI to obey their advice on what to do.

Forward-thinking businesses are beginning to invest significantly in Artificial Intelligence. When they begin to understand the application of AI to the industry deeply, they recognize the important impact of AI. With the rising digital disruption in all industries, AI must become a key and integrated component of its strategy.

The earlier businesses realize the effect of the changes brought on by Artificial Intelligence, the better positioned they would be to reap the benefits and face potential problems.

Cognitive Intelligence

Every human being has the ability to learn. Cognition is the way a person can assimilate, perceive the stimulus obtained from the external world. In order to develop cognitive intelligence, it is important to keep it working: living new experiences and learning, for example, are ways to stimulate it.

The simulation of cognitive intelligence in robots is being improved in AI. This means that algorithms are designed to provide machines with the ability to learn and adapt as they are used. Thus, the more a virtual assistant, for example, is enabled and communicates with users, the more "calibrated" it is. This optimizes the response and, as a result, the efficiency of the service.

Business Intelligence

Business intelligence is an extensive term that goes hand-in-hand with AI. It arose as a result of the competitiveness of companies combined with digital transformation. It is often referred to as the Business Intelligence acronym BI. It includes a series of ideas, best practices, and procedures in support of business performance. With this, Big Data, a robust database, is converted into valuable knowledge for the strategic use of organizations.

To this end, BI uses tools, such as management software, with applied artificial intelligence. With these services, businesses can make more precise analyses and therefore create more efficient strategic measures for business performance.

Artificial Intelligence in Human Resources

The consolidation of the highly strategic human resources market is leading to a fundamental transformation of its processes. Until recently, the field has been very tactical and is now becoming more analytical. The use of artificial intelligence in HR has thus established itself as a trend.

Mid and large businesses have recognized the relevance of Business Intelligence and Big Data to the department. They use these tools to increase their efficiency and performance. The use of software to handle HR processes is already a very lucrative business fact.

Artificial intelligence in HR is new but is already positioning itself as a clear strategic differentiation for high-performance management. According to data released by the Bain & Company consulting firm, 87 percent of the Human Resources leaders of major businesses expect digital technologies to change HR radically. Also, 57% of them are projected to raise their technology application budget in the sector by 2020.

The Human Resources Department is changing its structure and is now receiving more strategic managers. This trend is a result of the advent of People Analytics, which BI applied to people management. As a result, HR uses artificial intelligence to maximize its efficiency, guides the machines to take care of the operation, and prepares the team to assume analytical roles.

Data Visualization

For organizations that are still in the process of change and maturation, a meaningful way to start HR transformation is to use analytical management tools with data visualization. They allow managers to visualize area metrics using graphs, following the consolidation of Big Data with easier data manipulation. In addition, they are objectively visual, enabling the reading and interpretation of the data intuitively.

Human Resources Software

If your organization wishes to move forward, it is wise to use good management tools for the efficient routines of Human Resources. These systems ensure an operational transition to strategic HR by assuming, through artificial intelligence, process automation, and data consolidation.

What Are The Advantages Of HR's Artificial Intelligence?

The Department's routine tasks, such as attraction and selection of applicants, admission flow, payroll management, and even contact with employees, can be improved with artificial intelligence in HR and advanced software tools.

Experience Of Employees

By introducing People Analytics as the flagship of your strategic human resource management, you can enhance the employee's experience with your brand. For example, in an online selection process, the company values the applicant by encouraging their participation in the process. It is worth noting that we are in a crisis period. It is difficult for many candidates to pay travel costs for the selection process.

In addition, on-board data and employee travel must be focused on identifying discrepancies, enhancing training, developing more efficient methods for the transition of corporate culture, directly contributing to Employer Branding's success, and reducing turnover costs.

Fixed Cost Management

A further consequential advantage of AI is the optimization of fixed cost accounting in the field of human resources. In other words, with the data produced, it is possible to make more precise predictions, including the growth of the workforce. Through analyzing the patterns carried out by People Analytics, you can verify which times of the year and which industries have the highest turnover of employees so that you can forecast your fixed costs of human capital.

As a result, with artificial intelligence in HR, your company will be able to create solutions to process flow problems and even to the management of your leaders. High efficiency is thus achieved: cost savings and increased productivity. It is with the implementation of these internal and successful strategies that your company will progress towards success.

Artificial Intelligence in Retail

Optimization Of The Management Of Exposed Goods And Stocks

The technology known as computer vision is a groundbreaking AI-based method that enables computers to mimic human vision.

These solutions are now being used in the retail sector as an essential resource for managing the number of goods in stock and tracking items on gondolas and shelves.

Cameras equipped with this feature can detect when the product is out and send reminders to the buying department about the need for replacement.

Improved Customer Service

Tools such as the chatbot may be used to enhance customer communication with the shop. This function gives it control in the quest for a solution to its demands by presenting pre-programmed responses.

Chatbots simulate a personal service and offer more versatility to general doubts and objections. It is, therefore, possible to make the work done by human assistants more effective, as they can devote themselves to solving more complicated problems that are important to the results of the business.

Omnichannel service is also a feature that can be used in combination with chatbots. It makes the customer's relationship with the company more enjoyable by synchronizing different contact and service networks, improving the experience, enhancing organic marketing and loyalty.

Identification Of Patterns And Commercial Trends

AI's predictive capacity based on research and data analysis is another significant advantage for retail. Using intelligent software, it is possible to assess the evolution and usage trends per consumer and define those types of profiles that can be addressed more precisely by the sales team.

The increase or decrease in demand for a specific product is often quickly detected, providing the company with the information required to handle the procurement of new inputs for production or to adapt its business strategy according to its climate.

Greater Agility And Efficiency

Via AI, the managers responsible for the business, can access information on their various departments' results and improve them. Resources such as ERP integration tools may also be used in combination with AI in this respect.

Slow procedures, needless red tape, and repetitive activities can be avoided, for example, by the use of AI technologies used to evaluate purchase records, customer care, and goods monitoring. The results are more mobility and more production performance.

Automation Of Tasks

Artificial intelligence facilitates the automation of activities traditionally thought to be inefficient, leading to the reduction of repetitive behavior and exhaustion at work. Human resources are also best used in activities that are more important to the organization's core business.

The service provided by chatbots is also an example of this fact. Staff and sales teams will concentrate on achieving consumer recovery and service targets instead of only answering common questions that relationship robots can quickly answer.

Innovation And Differentiation Gains

The use of intelligent algorithms in combination with Big Data allows for greater access to relevant information. This can lead to insights into emerging products, new ways of delivering services, and new business opportunities.

In this way, AI can enhance creativity both in processes and in the supply of new products and services, allowing the business to distinguish itself and create a competitive edge.

Reducing High Costs

As we have shown, AI applications allow for reducing mistakes, the removal of bureaucratic processes, and the end of other inefficiencies through automation and better use of data analysis.

As a result, retail businesses that implement AI technology can put an end to waste and other costly operational costs. Therefore, the economic effects of profitability and the contribution margin are the most advantageous in this respect.

As you can see, a range of AI-based solutions is already available on the market. For this purpose, it is crucial to rely on the help of specialist companies in the industry to ensure that these solutions are implemented according to the profile and unique characteristics of your niche.

Artificial Intelligence in Banks

When we speak about the use of artificial intelligence in banks, the first solution that comes to mind is chatbots.

Obviously, this resource has encouraged and simplified banking systems, bringing more consistency to the services offered. However, the use of AI in financial services goes far beyond that.

According to the FEBRABAN Banking Technology Survey 2020, banks have increased their technology investments by 48 percent, including software and hardware.

Using AI, the approach focuses on enhancing the quality and creating more comfort for customers.

And when we speak about convenience, it is possible to mention the development of targeted financial products and services that have been built based on customer behavior research (done with the help of AI).

Artificial intelligence in banks also helps minimize costs, mitigate risks, and increase financial institutions' revenue.

In summary, it can be said that the primary goal of the use of artificial intelligence in banks is to enhance and reinforce the relationship between customers and financial institutions.

The almost immeasurable number of data produced daily by this sector gives its participants excellent opportunities to achieve this objective.

However, without the use of technology to refine this knowledge, this method is virtually impossible.

The use of artificial intelligence in banks makes it possible, among other things, to research customer behavior.

As a result, it is much easier to build financial products that really meet your needs based on actual facts.

In addition, AI has also been a valuable resource when it comes to reducing the costs of financial institutions.

Its implementation helps to optimize processes and increases the efficiency of internal sectors that do not have direct interaction with the customer but affect their relationship with the organization.

In short, the use of artificial intelligence in banks has become a major competitive differentiator.

One explanation is that the better you know the consumer and their needs, the more punctual the solution offering is to solve their problems.

This increases the attractiveness of the financial institution and thus increases its income.

AI also has a lot to do with banks and other businesses working in the financial sector. However, increased use can be seen in the following areas:

- Improvement of customer service
- Failed to reduce the cost of Backoffice
- Increased level of protection
- Providing more personalized products and services

Improvement Of Customer Service

According to FEBRABAN, the number of calls via chatbot increased by 258.5 percent between 2017 and 2018-three million calls were made in the first year, compared with 80.6 million in the second.

The use of a solution that uses and enhances natural language as it is used helps to enhance the customer's service experience and optimize this process.

Backoffice Cost Reduction

Beyond direct customer touch, artificial intelligence in banks has increasingly been used to improve the efficiency of internal industries, such as legal, on-boarding (opening accounts), among others.

AI helps to read and accept papers, procedures, and the like much quicker.

For example, digital accounts do not need the physical presence of the customer to be opened. However, digitally sent documents need to be validated.

Given the high opening volume of this form of account-7.4 million new digital accounts were opened in 2019. The more agile this process is, the better for the customer and the financial institution's reputation.

Increased Protection Standard

Any part of the study of consumer behavior and the use of artificial intelligence in banks is one of the best ways to do this.

AI is an integral part of detecting unusual customer profile behavior, particularly when combined with big data and analytics.

With this combination, it is possible to detect digital transactions that are incompatible with what is considered typical and therefore increase the degree of protection of the solutions provided.

Providing More Personalized Goods And Services

With this more in-depth study of consumer behavior, it is also possible, for example, to check the financial products that are most used, to perform a faster risk analysis to release credit to the customer, and much more.

This helps to provide genuinely differentiated products that address the current needs of this customer.

Here, it's worth noting that the arrival of Open Banking would make this whole offer even more ferocious.

With the exchange of bank data, the financial institutions that best manage to evaluate it and turn it into information will come forward.

With this in mind, it would be much simpler to deliver genuinely personalized solutions, emphasizing solving the client's current challenge and in an agile manner.

What To Expect From Banking Services In The Future

It is clear that the use of artificial intelligence in banks will grow well beyond the examples we have just mentioned.

For example, in the not too distant future, wearable items (wearable devices) will become very popular, leaving solutions such as cards and slips out of date.

The trend in the usage of technology in financial services is for the consumer to use the bank without understanding that they are using it.

CHAPTER 18
MYTHS ABOUT ARTIFICIAL INTELLIGENCE

Artificial intelligence, which was previously just a trend in futuristic fiction films, is now a fact for most businesses who want to become even more competitive on the market. With creativity and technology, these technologies automate some of the everyday activities and also reduce production costs.

Aware computers have been part of Hollywood literature for decades, creating concerns about the effects of technology. In reality, the rise of artificial intelligence and machine learning in recent years has not helped, and even people who should know better about it are giving in to fear. In any case, many of the negative feelings about AI come from the hyperactive imagination that computers will imitate our own bad behavior.

Apart from the films, there are some logical questions and answers on the subject. Let's split the myths and facts around AI and all its ramifications, including machine learning and deep learning.

Some sectors may be affected, and some jobs may be displaced, but this occurs on a continuous and daily basis. The industrial revolution of the late 19th century brought about massive changes. For example, the car left the horse industry out of the market.

"What's going to happen to people whose work will be replaced by AI? They're going to start doing other jobs. We've been doing this throughout human history. "This is nothing new," said David McCall, vice president of innovation for QTS data center operator.

"Based on all the work we're doing with large corporations, we're seeing a change in lower-level information staff," said Anthony DeLima, Head of Digital Transformation and US Operations at Neoris. "AI automates a number of activities performed by experts, runs 24 hours a day, 7 days a week, with a higher degree of precision, and also offers feedback and potential perspectives on where consumers or the business are heading," DeLima added. "So, in some situations, the amount of AI forecast exceeds what people can do."

Myth: Artificial Intelligence Machines Are More Intelligent Than Humans

Reality: AI is just as intelligent as the programmer is. "I think the smartest system in the world is the human brain, and we're not going to develop an AI that's smarter than it is. AI's not sentient, it's not awake, and I don't think it's smarter than we are," McCall said.

Without humans, there is no artificial intelligence. Human beings who are developing algorithms and knowledge that make up AI. We are building it, teaching it, and providing tools to make such decisions on our behalf.

"In some circles, AI can be used to make decisions faster than humans. This does not mean that decisions are always accurate, considered, or always deliver the right outcome," McCall said. "Is AI with a social conscience? Individuals can only take some decisions."

Myth: Artificial Intelligence For Information Technology Operationsis Is Primarily Focused On Event Management

Reality: It may be at the beginning, but it is changing.

"The initial wave of AIOps revolutionized our event management systems to eliminate noise based on related warnings, as in the cluster of similar alerts," said Ciaran Byrne, OpsRamp's vice president of product strategy. This was a significant move, as noise has long hindered the usability of event management systems.

But far more significant benefits are yet to come. "The next wave has been applied to other areas of IT operations, such as automation and monitoring/observability," Byrne said. "Applications will require smart ticket routing or automation based on learned trends."

Myth: Businesses Do Not Need An Artificial Intelligence Strategy

Reality: Ah, yes, you're going to need to.

QTS predicts that there will be no AI impact-free organization, sector, or market segment in the next decade. It is a dangerous proposition not to have an AI strategy because the competition will certainly-and they will be able to adapt much more quickly to market changes.

Jay Marwaha, CEO of SYNTASA, maker of behavioral analysis tools for consumer engagement and behavioral data, agrees. "The customers we work with believe that AI is the next major technology that businesses need to implement immediately to improve or reduce their profitability," he said.

How much AI effect depends on how businesses use it. Those who use AI for full impact are doing really well. "Some businesses don't understand the picture. They see the fashionable terms. They hear other businesses taking advantage of that," Marwaha explained. "The returns aren't always big, but in some cases, they're massive."

Myth: Artificial Intelligence Will Make Choices And Make Medical Diagnosis

Reality: Yes, but AI is not going to have the last word

Today, radiologists are specialists in assessing X-rays, MRIs, computed tomography, and other medical images. One of the primary efforts of AI is to teach image classifiers to identify anomalies such as tumors. AI has the potential to digitize millions of images and learn how to view knowledge faster and more thoroughly than any person could possibly do.

However, the doctor or radiologist will also have the final say on the diagnosis. The argument is that the diagnosis can be made in minutes instead of days or weeks.

Myth: We Don't Know What Artificial Intelligence Is Doing And Whether We Can Trust It

Reality: AI is a lot more transparent now

Initially, AIOps was seen as a "black box," that is, a mysterious device that produced results without providing details about what the underlying algorithm did and why. However, over time, we can see that these solutions have become more mature.

"While some systems do not provide clarity, more and more software providers and artificial intelligence systems are giving greater visibility to the reasons for the technology," said Byrne of OpsRamp. "The trick is to ensure sufficient clarity, not to overpower the customer, to gain their confidence and understanding."

Myth: I Need A Data Lake To Train Artificial Intelligence

Reality: it depends on that.

Unstructured data is worse than structured data since it takes up space. You need to use tools to filter to get rid of them. For that reason, McCall says, unstructured data can be useless.

"What the world is focused on now is how to arrange and organize data to manipulate it and how to construct algorithms," McCall said. "A bit of unstructured data is fine, but when we open gates, you need to have a data lake with the ability to organize and arrange it later."

Myth: Modeling Decides The Result

Reality: You can't be sure of that.

All AI initiatives start as test projects. You can get excellent results during the pilots but find that your model is much less reliable when used in development. This is because the AI and machine learning models must be data-trained. The training data must be reflective of the actual data-or the results will suffer the consequences.

Also, remember that preparation for your AI model is never going to be final. As soon as you put your model in the real world, its accuracy will begin to decline. The speed of the decline will depend on how rapidly real-world data changes (and consumer tastes will change quickly), but sooner or later, your model will need to be refocused with new details.

"It's a delicate job to identify the training data collection. Your training data must be the same as your output data," Marwaha said. "This is the secret to the success of your services."

And it's a key that you'll need to alter a few times in the life of your AI model.

Artificial Intelligence Works Like A Human Brain: MYTH

When it comes to artificial intelligence, equipment and systems may only perform the tasks assigned to them. For example, suppose an AI system has been created to diagnose computer problems. In that case, it is unlikely to be able to drive a vehicle.

This multidisciplinary character of the human brain is still far removed from the reality of artificial intelligence applications.

Artificial Intelligence Might Be Able To Assess The Competitiveness Of A Company: TRUTH

For organizations, adopting artificial intelligence to carry out specific day-to-day tasks is more than just modernity: it means a new internal framework. As this technology advances, fundamental changes can be observed in the efficiency of operations, job demands, and the business model.

For example, a company that uses AI with chatbots can automate various processes, including purchases, issuing and 2nd copy of slips, registration notifications, surveys, service assessment, among other various options. All of this affects the value of the business and, therefore, its success in the market.

Artificial Intelligence Will Replace Jobs: MYTH

In certain positions, the human element is indispensable because it is crucial to have a commitment, sympathy, vital sense, and other characteristics that are not present in artificial intelligence. As a result, AI may not be able to replace humans, particularly in jobs that require these qualities.

Artificial intelligence can only be used to automate such routine activities and assist the worker, such as data processing and web browsing assistance.

Artificial Intelligence Adapts To Various Market Types: TRUTH

One of the key benefits of artificial intelligence software is that it can adapt to different branches of industry, integrate with systems, and deliver solutions to different businesses. AI can be used, for example, by financial institutions, both in the area of customer service, conducting routine tasks such as credit data analysis and contracts.

Artificial intelligence often gains room when combined with drones, allowing a topographical analysis of certain complex regions to reach. Irrespective of business or need, an AI system promises to solve the problem and make the tasks even more realistic.

Let's all be calm, anyway! The good old "human intellect" is going to take a while to conquer!

CHAPTER 19

WHAT IS THE ACTUAL EFFECT OF ARTIFICIAL INTELLIGENCE ON COMPANIES?

Investing in artificial intelligence (AI) in the workplace and in the industry may sound like something for the future. Still, in many industries, it is already a reality.

According to the report "Getting Smarter by the Day: How AI Improves the Performance of Global Companies,"-made by Tata Consultancy Services with 835 executives, from 13 business segments located in four regions of the globe percent of organizations allocated at least US$250 million each to AI in 2016.

There was a connection between investment in AI and the effect on operations. Those with higher revenue gains and lower costs associated with an investment in AI have allocated five times more money to this technology than those with lower gains and lower costs associated with AI.

The champions had overall revenue growth of 16 percent in 2015 compared to 2014, while the others had a revenue increase of just 5 percent.

Want to know more about how AI can affect the future of work? Keep reading to find out about it!

What is the AI system?

The Artificial Intelligence System refers to a combination of multiple technologies (software, artificial neural networks, mechanisms, etc.) with a similar capacity to human thought and reasoning.

It enables a computer to experience, understand and interpret the world around it, to act on it based on its own decisions. The machine is also capable of learning on its own, thereby increasing its intelligence.

CHAPTER 20

HOW HAVE THE CORPORATE SECTORS BEEN AFFECTED?

Information Technology

According to Tata's survey results, the areas most embraced by AI are IT departments, with 67% of respondents using this technology to detect security intrusions, automation, and user issues.

But its potential does not stop there, as there are predictions that AI will replace many of the day-to-day functions in the IT sector, especially in operational areas. Among them, help desk, server management, and application support. Project management would also be affected.

This leads to the disappearance of some positions, but AI can optimize some skills gaps. Also, IT divisions will concentrate on more innovative work that generates differentials for organizations.

Marketing And Service

Marketing is one of the industries that could be affected by AI systems since they are capable of processing a large number of data from purchase interactions. In this way, in addition to predicting demands, it is possible to chart patterns and behaviors more precisely.

Artificial Intelligence can also be used in digital services, something that already exists with the use of IA chatbots, "Cousins"-only with reduced ability.

Financial

Thanks to its ability to process and interpret a vast amount of data, AI can play an essential role in analyzing credit and insurance grants and automating these activities.

Besides, it would be able to provide advice and recommendations so that managers can focus their decisions on enhancing the decision-making process concerning the economic resources of businesses.

From there, other financial metrics of the company can be improved based on more precise analyzes. This is the case with a reduction in the default rate, which can be minimized by a more effective and stable method of releasing credit to new customers.

Human Resources

One of the significant impacts of AI on HR is redirecting the workforce working in routine activities to higher value-added functions. This technology can begin to perform manual tasks that require less thought.

AI would also be able to free up time for HR workers by handling the long-term process of setting up new employees. There may also be the advent of an AI manager who can act to enhance the application and management of Artificial Intelligence within businesses.

According to research by the PwC Financial Services Institute, many executives see the prospect of enhancing employees' lives in AI managers.

Of the sum, 71 percent of the ears assume that employees would not mind working with an AI boss as long as it means getting more independence and flexibility to work at the home-a a popular home office. There will be no problems for 64 percent as long as this meant a much more manageable workload.

Which Segments Of The Market Have Been Affected?

Both the businesses that grow AI and those that take them into their operations will be able to profit from their ability, regardless of the field in which they find themselves.

According to one IDC/Salesforce report, by 2021, Artificial Intelligence's Customer Relationship Management (CRM) activities will increase business gains by US$1.1 trillion worldwide, creating 800 thousand new jobs that would help overcome those lost to automation.

AI is groundbreaking because it goes beyond mere mechanic automation. It includes cognitive processes. Its ability to learn enables it to perform activities that are not only routine and manual but also those involving reasoning and decision-making.

In this way, multiple segments can be affected, with very few constraints on the type of operation they conduct. Here are a few examples.

Logistics And Transport

The so-called self-driving cars are already at an advanced stage of growth, so that soon we will have AIs driving vehicles on roads around the world. They will be in a position to supply transport materials, among other logistical activities.

To make sense, major corporations, including Google, are leading the production of these vehicles, and they are also experimenting with Artificial Intelligence.

Legal

The ROSS Intelligence start-up program is able to look for processes in an enhanced way, include a list of the most relevant activities, and review events. This is thanks to AI-assisted cognitive computing developed by IBM, dubbed "Watson."

With this solution, just type in a computer topic, with a few paragraphs of text that can be returned hours later, full memos of several pages. It is worth remembering that the outcome has a solid basis and a clear legal language.

It can also filter a particular portion of the document that you want into more than a billion text documents. Most significantly, it knows the context of the decisions pursued and the rules, in addition to classifying data of interest and suggesting legal alternatives to professionals in the field.

Environment

IBM Watson is also being used to protect the environment, minimizing harm through its Artificial Intelligence. In this way, it is possible to forecast the environmental effects of works, consider the risks of various projects, and recommend decisions to reduce those risks.

All of this is focused on a large amount of data and statistics produced by computers, sensors, and other ecosystem monitoring tools.

Financial Institutions

Artificial Intelligence will be able to carry out large-scale operations requiring greater accuracy and efficiency in financial institutions, such as the rapid reconciliation of numerous mass transactions overnight.

The amount of data produced by financial institutions resulting from interactions with customers on their digital platforms increases exponentially every year in terms of volume and complexity. This offers a broad scope for us to evaluate knowledge better. Moreover, better understand customer desires, needs, and intentions.

How Professionals Are Going To Respond To These Changes?

AI is now being used to simplify processes and improve workflow productivity, allowing workers to be more efficient. It also helps them devote more time to strategic and innovative functions and create new jobs/services that have not been possible in the past.

This is true for the information technology industry. Analysts, technicians, and CIOS will face new challenges in the field, including adopting a more innovative and participatory position in the company's strategies.

In addition, the IT specialist would stand out as follows:

Preparing the market for innovation, that is, finding more creative and innovative solutions that enable the company to become more competitive;

To offer support to other agencies. In this situation, IT will also act as a bridge for other departments to be able to work with AI harmoniously and productively;

The programming of these systems and AI development will require many IT professionals trained in this technical field.

WHAT ARE THE ADVANTAGES OF INVESTING IN AI?

As you might imagine, artificial intelligence can offer advantages to businesses that plan to invest in this technology. Find out more about the advantages for specific industries in the following topics.

Relationship With The Customer

Artificial Intelligence is now being used to strengthen customer relationships, particularly about predicting demands and solving problems. The idea of cognitive computing in care is also discussed, which is capable of:

- understand human language;
- identify images;
- process questions and give quick responses.

It is the same resource used in chatbots that simultaneously supports many people, answers more straightforward questions, and offers specific guidelines for users.

Many businesses on Facebook already have this feature, providing a service menu. Depending on the demand, the robot itself is already able to address the issues posed.

Thus, it can be said that one of the critical benefits that AI provides in terms of quality is the ability to improve customer experience (especially concerning agility).

Sales And Marketing Services

The implications of using AI to enhance customer service contribute to better outcomes in the industrial and marketing sectors. In other words, if the public is more pleased with the company's buying experience, they will likely buy more.

One of the methods commonly used today to make this possible is Machine Learning. In Portuguese, it consists of an application in which systems learn to act based on analyzing the information collected.

Information Technology Security

Contrary to what many people believe, IT protection is one of the fields that benefits AI the most. It is the department that makes the most of the company's bets on this technology. The advantages here include:

- Prevention of attacks and other threats;
- Automation;
- A solution of problems;
- Proactive (rather than reactive) posture in the event of an attack;
- More accurate data-based decisions are welcome.
- Financial

Previously, humans' research work can now be done by algorithms with greater agility, reliability, and scalability. Furthermore, investing in artificial intelligence helps to improve security and avoid fraud in such transactions.

The idea is that AI often conducts more comprehensive and laborious tasks that would make it possible for practitioners to spend hours (or days) performing these activities. In return, they begin to devote more resources to strategic issues that add value to the company.

Data Analysis And Decision-Making

Many frameworks can integrate data and conduct, including analyzing knowledge, trends, and process execution time. From there, the tool already calculates (autonomously and automatically) the tables, indexes, and graphs that can be used in the management decision-making process.

AI-equipped computers are capable of learning from historical data and anticipating future behavior in the activities of employees (and also customers, assisting the commercial and marketing areas).

Also, they may estimate situations and determine the most suitable options for managers. In this way, it is possible to determine the plans and programs' capacity and degree of effectiveness before they are put into operation.

What Are The Critical Points To Be Noted?

Despite all the improvements and benefits that AI can bring to businesses and society as a whole, there are concerns about some important names in the field of technology. Check out the opinion of Elon Musk, Tesla and SpaceX's founder.

The work with Artificial Intelligence must be supervised

Musk claims that progress in the field is taking place very rapidly, with an exponential evolution. This means that we are close to the AI turning point-something that nobody expected to happen so quickly.

While learning progresses considerably, he believes that it is essential to ensure that this evolution takes place in synergy with the development of humanity. While he is not a steadfast supporter of the legislation, he acknowledges that this is the case, primarily because it entails risks for a large audience.

Therefore, there should be a body responsible for overseeing all those who securely create Artificial Intelligence.

Musk also argues that the threat posed by this technology is far greater than that posed by nuclear weapons. Since it would not be expected for people to produce nuclear weapons openly, neither should AI.

Investing in Artificial Intelligence is a growing trend that will revolutionize the business world, working primarily to solve well-defined and limited problems.

On the other hand, human beings would be critical in identifying what issues need to be addressed and resolving more complex challenges that require a high capacity for creativity and adaptability.

CHAPTER 21

ADVANTAGES AND DISADVANTAGES OF ARTIFICIAL INTELLIGENCE

Artificial Intelligence is one of the new technologies that attempt to replicate human reasoning in AI systems. In the year 1950, John McCarthy coined the word Artificial Intelligence.

He said, 'In theory, any aspect of learning or any other function of intelligence can be defined so precisely that a computer can be made to simulate it. An effort will be made to figure out how machines can use language, shape abstractions and definitions, solve the kind of problems now reserved for humans, and better themselves."

Artificial Intelligence is a computer program's ability to learn and think. Anything can be called Artificial Intelligence if it includes a program that does something that we would usually presume would rely on the intelligence of a human being.

The benefits of artificial intelligence systems are immense and will revolutionize every technical field. Let's see a few of them

Advantages

Human Error Reduction

The word "human error" was born because people make mistakes from time to time. Computers, however, do not make these errors if they are correctly programmed. With Artificial Intelligence, decisions are made based on previously collected knowledge using a series of algorithms. Thus, errors are minimized, and there is a chance of achieving accuracy with a higher degree of precision.

Example: The majority of human error was reduced in Weather Forecasting using AI.

Taking High-Risk Decisions

This is one of the main benefits of artificial intelligence. We can solve many of the risky limitations of humans by creating an AI Robot that can, in turn, do risky things for us. Let it go to March, dissolve a missile, explore the deepest parts of the oceans, mine coal and oil, and can be used effectively in any kind of natural or human-made catastrophe.

Example: Have you heard of the Chernobyl nuclear blast in Ukraine? At that time, there were no AI-powered robots that could help us mitigate the effects of radiation by managing the fire at an early point, as every human being was dead in a matter of minutes. Eventually, they pumped sand and boron out of helicopters from a distance. AI Robots can be used in conditions where the action may be dangerous.

Available 24/7

An average person would work 4–6 hours a day, excluding breaks. Humans are being designed in such a way as to get some time out to refresh themselves and get ready for a new day of work, and also to remain intact with their work-life and personal life on a weekly basis. But using AI, we can make machines work 24x7 without any breaks, and they don't get bored, unlike humans.

Example: Educational Institutes and Helpline Centers receive a range of inquiries and issues that can be effectively resolved through AI.

Assisting In Repetitive Work

In our day-to-day job, we're going to do much tedious work, including sending a thank-you mail, checking some error papers, and a lot more. Using artificial intelligence, we can productively automate these mundane tasks. We can also eliminate "boring" tasks for humans and set them free to become increasingly creative.

Example: In banks, we sometimes see many paperwork checks to get a loan. That is a tiresome process for the bank's owner. Using AI Cognitive Automation, the owner will speed up the process of checking the documentation that will help both the consumer and the owner.

Digital Support

Some highly advanced companies use digital assistants to communicate with users that save the need for human resources. Digital assistants have now been using several websites to deliver the things consumers want. We should talk to them about what we're looking for. Some chatbots are built to make it hard to find out that we're talking to a chatbot or a human being.

Example: We all know that companies have a customer service team that wants to clarify customer doubts and inquiries. Using AI, companies may set up a Voice Bot or Chatbot to assist consumers with all their queries. We can see that many companies have already started using them on their websites and mobile apps.

Faster Decisions

Using AI alongside other innovations, we can make machines take decisions faster than humans and take action more quickly. Although human decision-making can consider multiple variables both emotionally and functionally, the AI-powered computer operates on what is programmed and produces results more quickly.

Example: All of us played chess games on Windows. It's almost impossible to beat the CPU in the hard mode because of the AI behind the game. It will take the best possible move according to the algorithms used behind it in a short time.

Regular Applications

Daily apps like Apple's Siri, Window's Cortana, Google's OK Google are regularly used in our daily routine, whether it's location search, selfie, phone call, mail reply, and more.

Example: About 20 years ago, when we were preparing to go somewhere, we used to ask the person who went there for directions. But now, all we have to do is say, "OK Google, where Visakhapatnam is." It will show you the position of Visakhapatnam on the google map and the best route between you and Visakhapatnam.

New Inventions

AI is powering several inventions in almost every area to help humans solve most of the complex problems.

Example: Recently, physicians can predict breast cancer in a woman at an earlier stage using advanced AI-based technology.

As every bright side has a darker version of it. Artificial Intelligence also has many drawbacks. Let's see a few of them

Disavantages

High Development Costs

As AI upgrades every day, hardware and software need to be updated in time to meet the new requirements. Machines need to be repaired and maintained, generating high costs. Production needs massive costs since they are very complex machines.

Make Humans Lazy

AI makes humans lazy with its applications, automating much of the work. Humans appear to become addicted to these technologies, which can create problems for future generations.

Unemployment

As AI replaces the majority of routine activities and other robotic jobs, human intervention is becoming less and less likely to create a significant problem with job standards. Each enterprise seeks to replace the minimum eligible individuals with AI robots that can do similar work with greater efficiency.

Emotionless

There is no question that computers are a lot easier when it comes to operating effectively. Still, they cannot substitute the human interaction that makes the team. Machines cannot establish a relationship with humans, which is an essential trait for team management.

Lacking Different Approaches

Machines may perform only those tasks that they are designed or programmed to do, something out of which they appear to crash or offer meaningless outputs that could be extensive.

SUMMARY

These are some of the benefits and drawbacks of Artificial Intelligence. Any new technology or innovation would have both. Still, as people, we need to take care of it and use the optimistic side of the invention to make a better world. Artificial intelligence has enormous potential advantages. The human key will ensure that the "Rise of the Robots" does not get out of hand. Some people still argue that artificial intelligence will kill human civilization if it falls into the wrong hands. However, none of the AI applications made at that scale will kill or enslave humanity.

CHAPTER 22

APPLICATION OF ARTIFICIAL INTELLIGENCE IN DAILY LIFE

As time passes, it is more frequent that artificial intelligence facilitates the things we do on a regular basis.

The notion that robots are conquering the world seems to be something out of a science fiction film or, at the very least, something that will not be a reality until, say, 2035. But the truth is different: now is the future.

Artificial intelligence applications have been around for decades, often in ways much more mundane than driving cars or facial recognition technology. Intelligent technology does so many things behind our backs, and that we don't really see that we'd be shocked to find out how hard our lives will be without it.

Examples of How AI is Already in our Everyday Life

1. VOICE ASSISTANTS

In today's houses, people love to have smart speakers and voice assistants. According to a new survey by Nielsen, only reviewing the situation in the United States, 24 percent of households have smart speakers, such as Google Home or Amazon Echo. Using natural language processing (NLP) to interpret and respond to voice commands, these assistants allow you to play music with an order, remind you to throw away the garbage, or read a goodnight story to your children.

2. SMARTPHONES

Smartphones use AI in several respects, so you're sure to use it with only one finger a few times a day. Siri and Google Assistant are already standard mobile phone functions that allow you to conduct voice searches and queries. Also, the intelligent changes made to the "selfies," that is, what happens when you use the portrait mode of your iPhone, are made through artificial intelligence that identifies the proper focus.

3. CONTENT OF SOCIAL NETWORKS

If you enjoy tweeting, are addicted to Instagram, or are a mega user of Facebook, most of the messages and content you get from social networks are artificially intelligent. Your user interface is entirely tailored to your needs. Each platform gives you the details you think you're searching for, so you'll come back more, so the next time you spend hours reading the news, you'll know why.

4. GOOGLE PREDICTIVE

If you use Google as a search engine, you might have found that it gives you a suggestion to complete a question based on your written text. The data from this predictive search is provided based on the data that Google gathers about you (and other users) as you visit the internet, such as your age, location, and other personal data. The search engine uses AI to predict what you may be searching for and thus be able to provide you with better knowledge.

5. RECOMMENDATION OF PRODUCTS

Sellers like Amazon use artificial intelligence to gather knowledge about your buying habits and preferences so that they can customize your online experience. These items are recommended based on your habits and interests so that you feel like you're shopping with the aid of an online personal assistant. It's not shocking that we replay the feeling over and over again.

6. CUSTOMER SERVICE

Chatbots enable thousands of customers from all industries to get answers to basic questions or help with technical support. For example, a banking entity's chatbot will handle questions and basic requests, such as displaying the balance available, transferring funds, and closing accounts. Bots use AI to help consumers search for data. Still, they also provide benefits because they can store consumer usage data and offer products based on their individual needs.

7. MUSICAL RECOMMENDATIONS

Who doesn't want to have specific playlists based on their musical preferences? Artificial intelligence services such as Spotify and Alexa learn the diverse tastes and musical preferences of these application users to create better playlists. Data such as the length of an album, tone, or genre can allow these platforms to recommend similar songs and artists to their users.

8. MAPS AND DIRECTIONS

AI also has a vital role to play in navigation systems. Suppose you're using Google or Apple Maps to get directions. In that case, artificial intelligence reads many data points so that users can get up-to-date and real-time traffic status information. Voice navigation lets drivers follow the most effective path, and some navigation interfaces also recommend routes to popular locations.

9. HOME AUTOMATION

Enter the house without the keys and switching the lights on only by using the voice are circumstances that are becoming more widespread in today's households, all thanks to artificial intelligence. There are complete protocols like Z-Wave that enable homeowners to build their own Internet of Things (IoT). Using "low-frequency radio waveform," Z-Wave smart home devices can communicate with each other and with other applications to automate processes that previously required human contact. There's no longer any need to keep battling with a frustrating programmable thermostat-let it program itself!

10. SPAM FILTERS

Email service providers are increasingly using artificial intelligence to filter spam, and users are pleased. Instead of clicking a spam report icon, Gmail and other email services use machine learning to differentiate between legitimate emails and those that are not. Also, each user has different preferences, so the AI can help you customize your mailbox.

11. AGRICULTURE

Agriculture is one of the oldest practices of humankind. Some procedures, in many places, are carried out in an archaic manner.

On the other hand, several businesses have invested in technology to improve efficiency and reduce costs and losses. Artificial Intelligence is just one of them.

We are talking about 'smart agriculture,' where farmers are starting to cultivate with more sustainability and productivity, track production, and reduce risks. In agriculture, machines can learn how to identify soil issues, produce statistical data and help planters make decisions on planting, harvesting, and selling.

It is essential to say that AI research does not stop and that new facilities and possibilities are emerging every day. An example of this is 3D printers, which have been gradually improved to be used in different fields, from health (manufacturing of human organs, for example) to industrial development (creation of parts quickly and without errors).

12. FINANCIAL MARKET

Artificial Intelligence has also been of great benefit in the field of finance. Investors may rely on a multitude of applications and software, for example, to help them organize finances and even invest.

Besides, thanks to Artificial Intelligence and technology development, even investment operations on the stock exchange are possible. Humanly, it would be challenging to keep up with all the stock market movements, so intelligent robots do it.

Startups cannot be ignored either. After all, some robots search for investment alternatives and show the investor's profile. The output of each portfolio is tracked, and changes can also be made via AI.

Have you seen how Artificial Intelligence is more present in our everyday lives than we can imagine? And, do you have any idea how Artificial Intelligence can be used to better your everyday life?

CHAPTER 23
ARTIFICIAL INTELLIGENCE FOR HUMANOID ROBOTS

Do you think you're smart? Ok, because? Believe me, the answer to that question is a lot more complex than you can imagine. It is possible to characterize intelligence as the ability to consider and solve new problems and conflicts and to adapt to new situations. In this sense, it is only by being able to solve the problem of answering a query that you are already considered intelligent. But this concept is so broad that it is challenging to assign knowledge solely to human capacity. For example, most animals can change their actions at various stages, depending on the adversity they face.

Thus, we may take the idea of intelligence to a different dimension, defining it as a trait not only of individuals but also of structures. An intelligent machine must be able to identify the state in which it is located, assess the possibilities for action, and decide on how to proceed based on its objective. You may not have noticed, but you are likely to be in contact with intelligent systems on a daily basis through mobile devices and personal computers. In computing, artificial intelligence can be described as the study of intelligent agents – the essential components of an intelligent system.

One of the areas of application of artificial intelligence in robotics. Robots, equipped with artificial intelligence, can help people perform more complex tasks and are more effective than those without such functionality, thereby increasing the efficiency and comfort of their owners. Humanoid robots have been created that mimic human beings in appearance to extend human emotion to robots, taking them closer to a familiar physiognomy.

One of the significant milestones in the development of this field occurred in October 2017, when Sophia, a gynoid created by Hanson Robotics, was the first robot to gain citizenship from Saudi Arabia. It was developed to adapt to and interact with human beings in the future.

Artificial intelligence algorithms focusing on natural language processing (NLP) and recognizing human features, such as gestures, facial expressions, and speech, have been introduced to make this possible. These techniques allow Sophia to have more realistic experiences with people. In addition to interpreting these signals, she can also replicate gestures, expressions, and tones of voice relevant to the communication context.

In addition to becoming a resident, Sophia became famous thanks to videos of her interviews on television shows. However, other humanoid robots have been popular a long time before that. Japanese car manufacturer Honda has been investing in robotics since the 1980s. Its robot, ASIMO (Advanced Step in Innovative Mobility), is one of today's most advanced humanoid robots.

ASIMO began to evolve in 1986. The engineers of the time were looking to build a robot capable of reproducing a human being's surface. At present, he is in a more advanced stage of progress, performing different kinds of movements, such as walking, running, and jumping. With cameras that act as eye and image processing algorithms, ASIMO can understand the world in which it finds itself and adjust its motion to different circumstances. Also, he can respond to simple voice commands and recognize the faces of some individuals.

Today, ASIMO is a source of inspiration for students from various schools around the world. The robot is brought to institutions to stimulate the interest of boys and girls in the acquisition of scientific knowledge by promoting the study of mathematics, physics, anatomy, and, of course, robotics.

A variety of organizations are researching the field of robotics in parallel with Honda engineers. Another prominent example in the media is robotics created by a group born at the Massachusetts Institute of Technology (MIT) known as Boston Dynamics. Via a YouTube channel, the organization disseminates the progress of its study, showing the success of robots in a series of supervised tests.

Boston Dynamics has a range of robot models with different features and different artificial intelligence techniques, such as Handle, SpotMini, Atlas, and Spot. They all work with recognition algorithms to create maps of the paths they know and recognize the obstacles surrounding them. From this info, you can walk, run, jump and even climb the stairs!

Artificial intelligence is essential for movement in open space and replicating human movements or facial expressions, as seen in the robots described. Still, it is possible to go beyond that. Recently, computational models have been created to construct their own mental map of how to interpret the world when applied to humanoid robotic bodies. The iCub is the robot that exemplifies this.

ICub

To better understand how cognitive processes function in us humans, iCub has been built so that its way of learning is similar to that of a child. This android has sensors that replicate our senses of sight and hearing. With supervised machine learning algorithms, it can process the information obtained by the sensors and form connections between the words spoken by the individual and the images presented. This is possible because when iCub is studying, a person says when they do the correct association. With each hit, he reinforces the connection and, with each error, recombines the details, trying to get it right the next time.

Robots who learn how iCub is very useful for the computer sector, as data capture in real-time during both the training and testing phases enables contact with the environment to be closer to what we humans have. Perhaps it is the catalyst of a great revolution that aims to benefit our society, unlike many science fiction works.

At present, some robots operate with telepresence. That is, they are powered by the link with the user and manipulated by his movements. For example, Da Vinci, a robotics project applied to medicine that was launched in 2006 in the USA, is a robot (not a humanoid, in this case) that performs extremely delicate surgeries with great precision and without tremors. The device is currently operated remotely by a surgeon. With developments in this field, it would be possible to introduce Artificial Intelligence algorithms that allow these robots to work independently, save effort, and be generated on a large scale. For example, the Da Vinci system could save many lives.

AI and Robotics are two fields that have developed a lot in recent years and have a very fascinating and little-explored intersection. Every year, artificial intelligence systems impress us with their performance. The robots that implement them are emerging at a rapid rate. There will definitely be many studies and projects that will surprise us even more. Developers of these ventures will also need to resolve ethical problems. Still, the future looks very positive, and society will eventually reap the benefits of these advances. After all, if the technology does not benefit humans, what would be the purpose of developing it?

CONCLUSIONS

AI has been at the forefront of computer science since the 1950s and has been a subject of interest, especially in terms of patenting. This study includes 85,144 AI inventions patented worldwide between 1998 and 2017. Approximately 2% or 1,516 patented AI inventions are affiliated with Canadian researchers and institutions. Breaking this Canadian subset further, we find 618 AI inventions involving at least one Canadian institution and 1,419 inventions involving at least one Canadian researcher. Overall, Canada ranks sixth in terms of the amount of raw patented innovations, either from the point of view of researchers or organizations.

On an international stage, China and the United States are leading the AI race. In 2011, the surge in AI patented innovations changed the landscape, most of which originated in China. Computer Vision and NLP are the AI Applications responsible for most of the activities. At the same time, Life and Medical Sciences and Transportation are the most proprietary AI Fields. ML overshadows all other techniques, both domestically and abroad, when they pertain to AI Techniques.

There are many hubs of interest in this sector in Canada. Each of the superclusters offers nurturing environments for emerging talent, focusing on the industries local to those specific geographic areas. This creates activity centers, each with its own specialization, as can be seen from the CMA cluster map presented in the Canadian Institutions section. Other programs that have been placed in place in Canada include the Equitable AI Initiative and the Canada–UK Initiative, each focused on different objectives for the advancement of foreign and domestic cooperation, ethics, and AI policy. Also, Canada has established a Pan-Canadian Artificial Intelligence Strategy. This $125M project brings together major players in the sector to ensure cooperation, equity, and economic advancement.

As far as AI Fields is concerned, Canada has highly specialized in Physical Sciences and Engineering and Life and Medical Sciences, two of the most proprietary AI Fields. However, one field in which Canadian innovation could stand to benefit is Transportation, where its relative specialization is far behind the rest of the world. In terms of AI Applications, Canada is more diversified than the U.S., where the latter excels in NLP and Computer Vision compared to the other subcategories of AI Applications.

The gender ratio worldwide, as it relates to the distribution of researchers involved in patented AI innovations, is one female for every three males. This ratio is one female for every six males in Canada. This disparity cannot be clarified simply by the ratio of graduates in engineering or science, except instead by hints of alternative explanations. The Canadian Department for Women and Gender Equality has put forward a range of proposals to impact young women in the pursuit of further, and feel secure staying in these positions and raising the ranks of these organizations. IP recognition will be a welcome addition to these initiatives.

As the AI technology sector continues to develop and evolve, it is crucial to notice the challenges facing AI in Canada, particularly the retention of talent and institutions. The first-come, first-serve essence of the AI industry makes it highly competitive when it comes to investor financing. The findings also confirm the level of rivalry on the AI market in Canada, as validated by the IPCI results. Canadian investment trends engage more existing firms than companies in their first round of funding instead of the U.S. Footnote 44. This disparity in financing methods reflects the high rate of acquisition by American companies of Canadian institutions. Looking forward, it will be essential to see how Canada adapts to the rapidly changing nature of AI and how organizations can utilize their IP to support business decisions and development. However, as AI is better described and understood, it can be predicted that it will be gradually governed both domestically and abroad. Still, at present, there are many opportunities for players to set standards and affect the pace at which this technology is applied in our daily lives.

www.ingramcontent.com/pod-product-compliance
Lightning Source LLC
Chambersburg PA
CBHW062107220526

45471CB00010B/3632